BEFORE AND AFTER

TENNESSEE CHILDREN'S HOME SOCIETY
SHELBY COUNTY BRANCH

MISS GEORGIA TANN
Assistant State Superintendent

TELEPHONE 8-7355
614 GOODWYN INSTITUTE BUILDING
MEMPHIS
TENNESSEE

May 21, 1936

Mr. and Mrs.
Springdale
Arkansas

My dear Mr. and Mrs.

     We have a baby boy we believe you will be interested in and since the Worker has to make a visit to your home before a placement can be made we ask that you send transportation to the amount of $14.00, bus fare and incidentals. She will bring the baby to you and if you are entirely satisfied we leave the baby. If not, the Worker will return him to the organization.

     Kindly let us hear from you at an early date,

Yours very truly,

Georgia Tann

Georgia Tann,
Asst. State Superintendent

Before and After

THE INCREDIBLE REAL-LIFE STORIES OF ORPHANS WHO SURVIVED THE TENNESSEE CHILDREN'S HOME SOCIETY

Judy Christie and *Lisa Wingate*

BALLANTINE BOOKS

NEW YORK

Copyright © 2019 by IMWW LLC and Monday House LLC

Published in the United States by Ballantine Books, an imprint of Random House, a division of Penguin Random House LLC, New York.

BALLANTINE and the HOUSE colophon are registered trademarks of Penguin Random House LLC.

Photo credits are located on page 293.

LIBRARY OF CONGRESS CATALOGING-IN-PUBLICATION DATA

NAMES: Christie, Judy Pace, author. | Wingate, Lisa, author.

TITLE: Before and after : the incredible real-life stories of orphans who survived the Tennessee Children's Home Society / Judy Christie and Lisa Wingate.

DESCRIPTION: First edition. | New York : Ballantine Books, [2019]

IDENTIFIERS: LCCN 2019034565 (print) | LCCN 2019034566 (ebook) | ISBN 9780593130148 (hardcover) | ISBN 9780593130155 (ebook)

SUBJECTS: LCSH: Tennessee Children's Home Society—Corrupt practices—History. | Adoption agencies—Corrupt practices—Tennessee—History. | Family reunification—Tennessee—Case studies.

CLASSIFICATION: LCC HV875.56.T2 C47 2019 (print) | LCC HV875.56.T2 (ebook) | DDC 362.73092/2768—dc23

LC record available at https://lccn.loc.gov/2019034565

Printed in the United States of America on acid-free paper

randomhousebooks.com

9 8 7 6 5 4 3 2 1

FIRST EDITION

Book design by Barbara M. Bachman

For the heroes of these stories:

the adoptees and their families

Where are you? Do you look like me?

Are you like me in any way?

—LETTER FROM A TENNESSEE
CHILDREN'S HOME SOCIETY
ADOPTEE TO HER UNKNOWN
BIRTH FAMILY

CONTENTS

FROM THE AUTHORS

————

THESE STORIES ARE AS REMEMBERED AND GENEROUSLY told by Tennessee Children's Home Society adoptees and their families. To respect their privacy, we have changed the names of adoptees and family members, with the exception of wonderful actors Stephen Smiley Burnette, his daughter, Elizabeth, and his parents, the incomparable Smiley and Dallas Burnette.

————

IN OUR HEARTS, WE WILL ALWAYS HOLD SACRED THE TRUE names of each of the people we have gotten to know through their stories.

PROLOGUE

———

JULY 1950 IS A HOT, UNEASY MONTH IN WEST TENNESSEE.
The United States enters the Korean War. Fear of a third
world war hovers while the region still grapples with the after-
effects of the second one. The stock market plunges. As if that
is not enough, boll weevils plague cotton crops and devastate
farmers trying to eke out a living.

Tumult of a different sort, though, brews for a young pregnant woman. She has been sent out of state with her three-
year-old son, her sister, and a nephew to await the birth of her
second child.

A house is provided. Expenses taken care of.

But the largesse comes at a high price.

She has agreed to hand her baby over to Georgia Tann, who
has run a questionable orphanage in Memphis for more than
twenty-five years. Rumors about Tann's toxic adoption practices swirl like a hot wind on a dusty day, and they are about to
hit gale force.

Tann's empire at the Tennessee Children's Home Society—
shortened to TCHS by those familiar with the operation—has
been built with a combustible blend of desperate pregnant

women, shattered children, vulnerable poverty-stricken families, eager adoptive parents, powerful politicians, ego, and greed.

But this young mother's life is complicated, and Tann offers a solution.

A sweet baby girl is born on Monday, July 10, 1950.

Five days later, a TCHS worker whisks the newborn away. The traumatized mother is left behind with her preschool-age son. The baby girl will not see her brother again for four decades. The aunt, who has come along as a companion on this sad journey, will keep the secret from family and friends back home, intending to take it to her grave.

On July 26, the infant is delivered to a new set of parents—a couple with turmoil of its own.

Scarcely two weeks old, the tiny girl is on a path that will shape everything she becomes. Whisked away with the speed of a wartime ballistic missile, she will spend most of her life piecing together the mystery of her birth and early years . . . and wondering how things might have been different.

TENNESSEE CHILDREN'S HOME SOCIETY
SHELBY COUNTY BRANCH

MISS GEORGIA TANN
Assistant State Superintendent

TELEPHONE 6-7333
514 GOODWYN INSTITUTE
BUILDING
MEMPHIS
TENNESSEE

May 21, 1936

Mr. and Mrs.
Springdale
Arkansas

My dear Mr. and Mrs.

We have a baby boy we believe you will be interested in and since the Worker has to make a visit to your home before a placement can be made we ask that you send transportation to the amount of $14.00, bus fare and incidentals. She will bring the baby to you and if you are entirely satisfied we leave the baby. If not, the Worker will return him to the organization.

Kindly let us hear from you at an early date,

Yours very truly,

Georgia Tann

Georgia Tann,
Asst. State Superintendent

PART ONE

Truth Meets Fiction

CHAPTER 1

REAL-LIFE ADOPTEES

"Have you considered a reunion?"

ONNIE WILSON IS RELAXING IN HER CONDO IN SOUTHERN California with her beloved Labradoodle, Jackson, when the email arrives.

"Oh my gosh, Connie!" a book-club friend from Arizona writes. "Have you read *Before We Were Yours?*"

It's June 2017, and the novel by Lisa Wingate is brand-new. Connie has not heard of it. But faster than her pup can nudge her to play tug-of-war, she downloads a digital copy. In only forty-eight hours, she devours it, tamping down emotions as she reads. The fictionalized story about children adopted through the Tennessee Children's Home Society is oh so familiar to her.

Connie's life is historic in a way she would rather have avoided: she is one of the last babies placed by the scandal-ridden orphanage. In her late sixties when she, Lisa, and I meet, Connie is one of the youngest members of a unique and uncomfortable club—living adoptees connected to TCHS. People whose lives were irrevocably altered at the hands of Georgia Tann. For Connie and thousands like her, events that took place decades ago are difficult to place in the past. The effects remain ever present.

On September 11, 1950, just two months after Connie's birth, a criminal investigation into Tann's adoption practices was announced. Orphanage funds were cut, and the babies on hand were left in limbo. Connie's adoption was held up, and her guardianship was transferred from TCHS to the Tennessee Department of Public Welfare. That was when she joined the tail end of a decades-long line of sad statistics.

Under the autocratic control of Georgia Tann, and thanks to her effective grip on look-the-other-way political and civic leaders, TCHS managed to operate in Memphis from 1924 to 1950 without scrutiny or interference. Approximately five thousand children, many of whom were not actually orphaned, passed through the agency's doors. An unknown number, estimated at five hundred, perished in unregulated, often squalid, holding facilities. Others were delivered into homes that faced little to no scrutiny, to parents who, for a host of reasons, could not adopt conventionally.

These real-life stories left their mark on ordinary people, now in the final season of their lives, as they pass along their experiences with TCHS and Tann's deeds to future generations through their personal accounts of what happened . . . and through their DNA.

A blend of what was happening in the world, from the Great Depression to World War II and the Holocaust, and including the stigma of unwed motherhood, led to the growth of Tann's network for obtaining and placing children. Poverty-stricken mothers gave up babies out of desperation; unmarried young women were not allowed to keep their newborns because of the taint of illegitimacy; and poor parents, hard at work, often unable to afford babysitters, found their children lured from front yards and into Tann's chauffeur-driven black limousine as it glided around Tennessee and Arkansas. With her paid network of doctors, social workers, and even boardinghouse owners, Tann snatched babies up as soon as they became available.

This photograph of Georgia Tann in the parlor of the orphanage was included in one of the home's marketing brochures for prospective parents.

Some frantic birth parents—along with the occasional physician—attempted to challenge Tann, a stern-looking woman with short hair and glasses. Tann, however, had political clout and immense wealth, built on the backs of children sold for profit, some of it from checks made out to her personally. With the help of her connections via Memphis mayor E. H. "Boss" Crump, a political kingpin with powerful ties throughout the state, and others in positions of authority, she deflected inquiries with the ease of swatting a mosquito on a Tennessee summer afternoon.

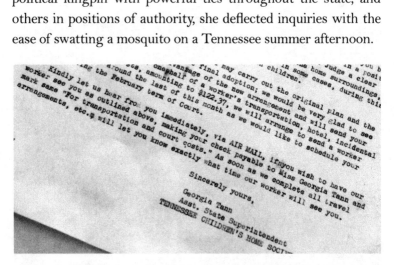

Georgia Tann writes adoptive parents and asks for reimbursement, with checks made payable to her personally.

But now, in 1950, the year of Connie's birth, the end of Tann's reign of terror nears. Tennessee politics are changing. Crump is out. The new Tennessee governor, Gordon Browning, appoints attorney Robert Taylor to ferret out the grisly truth of TCHS's Memphis operations. He has already discovered damning evidence. Only a small network of co-conspirators know the truth. With the investigation under way, they flee into the crevasses of Memphis and disappear like rats running into the city's sewers. Although some community leaders—powerful, wealthy, political—have undoubtedly been complicit, all the blame is conveniently assigned to Tann.

She holes up in her home, reportedly in the last stages of uterine cancer—too ill, it is said, to respond to the charges or face the public. Governor Browning releases Taylor's shocking initial report, which details Tann's years of nefarious dealings in the adoption market. She has, the governor reveals, made herself rich and completed an unknown number of horrendous deals involving flesh-and-blood products.

Within days, on September 15, 1950, it is announced that she has died. Tann, fifty-nine, never married, leaves her estate to her mother, an adopted daughter, and an adopted sister. The orphanage is not mentioned. The Tennessee State Legislature quickly and quietly seals the paperwork of thousands of TCHS children, which will leave adoptees desperately searching for decades to uncover the truth about their heritage. The investigation concludes that Tann profited from the operation of TCHS in Memphis in excess of five hundred thousand dollars in the last ten years of her life—taking in today's equivalent of between five and ten million dollars.

During that period, the investigation found, she placed more than a thousand children for adoption outside the state of Tennessee, principally in New York and California, the exact number not known.

If Connie, the baby girl born just two months before Tann's death, and these thousands of other children were characters in a novel, justice as well as blame might have landed squarely on Tann's head. Police would swoop into her Memphis Receiving Home, rescue her remaining charges, shackle Tann, and whisk her off to jail. She would endure a trial and be forced to stand eye to eye with children she procured in the 1920s or 1930s or 1940s, or with parents whose babies were snatched, or with people in California and New York who paid extra for children because they sensed that if they didn't, their in-process adoptions might suddenly go wrong.

But real life does not happen that way.

Tann dies, never having admitted to her crimes and, supposedly, never having known that she has finally been exposed, and certainly not having paid back the money that supported her lavish lifestyle. She is never made to face families she misused, those good and kind people who will spend a lifetime unraveling the knots she tied, a lifetime trying to heal the hearts she broke.

But finally, all these years later, her name is ruined, her power gone. Now the triumph belongs to quiet conquerors, who are ready to tell *their* stories.

In a piece of history with so many villains, they are the heroes.

STILL IN THE THROES of reading *Before We Were Yours*, Connie is intrigued when her book-club friend surfaces again with an invitation: "Would you mind talking about you and the book?"

A seasoned traveler after years in the business world, Connie happily makes plans to hop a plane to Arizona a couple of months later. Spurred on by this interest in her past, she emails the author of the novel, a woman she has never met.

09/12/17 AT 4:06 P.M.

Dear Lisa Wingate,

Reading your new book *Before We Were Yours* inspired me to go back through all the records, articles, and information I have gathered about my adoption . . .

I was reunited with my natural brother after 40 years of not knowing I even had one (same for him). It is a wonderful story if you are interested. I also think you would find interesting all the letters from Georgia Tann and the research for the 40 years that followed.

I'd also love to know how the other victims are today. What emotional impact this had on them.

Please let me know if you'd like me to come speak with you, bring any records, or just have a phone call.

Looking forward to
hearing from you,
Connie

Lisa is crisscrossing the United States on a book tour when the note lands in her swollen email inbox. The idea of an in-person meeting draws her, but the novel is only weeks old. With stops on her publicity tour from New York City to Los Angeles, she can scarcely keep up with what time zone she's in. She will ponder the logistics later, when she can settle into her favorite writing chair with her cherished dog, Huckleberry, and sleep in her own bed.

But as the miles add up, so do emails from other adoptees and their family members. *Before We Were Yours* stirs an unanticipated response from real-life older adults who have lived with so many questions and too few answers—and from their children and grandchildren, who carry DNA mysteries of their own.

Aging adoptees seem compelled, often in understated ways, to talk about what happened when their childhoods were redirected by Tann. Even those with the most positive adoptive experiences recall agonizing moments. Many others speak of homes filled with drama and heartache. Some describe unthinkable experiences, both in Tann's horrific system of holding facilities and in unvetted adoptive homes.

After all these years, many remain, in ways, incomplete.

Their emails reveal deeply personal experiences and haunting quests pursued along lonely paths. They volunteer stirring real-life stories:

> My brother was taken from a hospital. My mother was told he died.
> I was shipped to Hollywood.
> My birth mother was Irish-Catholic, but my adoptive parents were Jewish.

They ask heartrending questions:

> Was my mother selling her children?
> Could I have been stolen as an infant?
> How could this have happened?
> Why didn't anyone stop it?

Packets of information with detailed adoption records wait in Lisa's post-office box when she returns home. Among them, the compilation of information about Connie's forty-year effort to unravel the mystery of her adoption.

Lisa, on and off the road, and in the middle of a family relocation back to her home state, answers Connie's question about a visit:

09/15/17 AT 10:35 P.M.

Hi Connie,

I would love to set up a time to talk with you and yes, I'd love to work out a time to get together, hear about your memories . . . and also look through the rest of your records. I've heard so many wonderful stories of family reunions since starting on this project, and, of course, some sad stories as well.

I will email after things settle down around mid-October and we'll set up a time to talk!

Warmly,
Lisa

September rushes into October. Life in the Wingate household tumbles end over end. The eldest son has recently married, and a new daughter-in-law joins the family. Lisa's youngest son has graduated from college, landed an engineering job, and is navigating the world of housing, insurance forms, and employment paperwork. There's motherly advice to give, and pots, pans, furniture, and pillows to sort for a fledgling apartment. And the son is not the only one headed to a new nest. A moving van travels to a fixer-upper house in Texas, where Lisa's husband has started a new teaching job. The Wingate stint in temporary lodging in a loft space over a coffee shop is drawing to a close.

Before We Were Yours has catapulted into readers' hands, propelled by word of mouth, through reader-to-reader and book-club-to-book-club recommendations. Not only has the novel affected adoptees and family members hungry to know more, it grabs book lovers around the world as it is published in foreign-language editions in thirty-five countries. The abuse of children, sadly, isn't just an American issue, but one that travels across cultural boundaries.

While chaos is reigning in Lisa's world, Connie experiences a new world of her own. One she never anticipated. In Anthem, Arizona, the book-club discussion of *Before We Were*

Yours begins enthusiastically—and continues for three and a half hours. Readers fling questions at her, curious, angry at what happened, inspired by her courage. Then an unexpected question comes. "One gal said, 'Have you ever considered doing a reunion?'" Connie recalls. Of course she has considered it. She *yearns* for it. At the book club, this idea that has resided in her heart floats about the room, out in the open for everyone to see.

When she returns home, she emails Lisa with an update. And another question:

10/18/17 AT 11:16 A.M.

Dear Lisa,

I was invited to join my old book club to discuss *Before We Were Yours* and my own experience with Georgia Tann . . . Everyone was so interested in your characters and the true story of those who were separated.

Would you ever be interested in doing a reunion with these victims? I was a senior vice president of a company and did a lot of event planning. I would be happy to help put something together, if you are in the least bit interested?

Your book really pushed me to dive back into the history of my past.

Best wishes,
Connie

Wrapping up a leg of the book tour and touched by these true stories, Lisa is increasingly drawn to the idea of a reunion.

These adoptees—survivors really—deserve *something*. But what? The logistics seem daunting. With the death of adoption rights champion Denny Glad, a Memphis resident who helped connect adoptees like Connie with their birth families, and the end of Tennessee's Right to Know project, which fought to open Tennessee's adoption records for decades, finally succeeding in 1995, there is no clearinghouse for TCHS adoptees and family members. No convenient place to go with unanswered questions. Nowhere to compare paperwork, share stories, meet others drawn into this aging group of survivors.

Lisa, unable to shut the reunion door, gets back in touch:

10/19/17 AT 10:10 P.M.

Dear Connie,

I love your idea of doing some sort of reunion gathering of victims. These stories should be validated and shared. Thank you for offering to help. It sounds like you have just the right expertise for this sort of thing.

In the meantime, I'm cataloging stories and contacts as I hear from people who are connected to TCHS.

Warmly,
Lisa

Nudges for a reunion come in trickles . . . and then a torrent. *Before We Were Yours* is chosen as the "If All Arkansas Read the Same Book" selection for 2018. Lisa will tour the state in the spring. That's *Arkansas*, next door to Tennessee. Just across the river from Memphis. Another invitation for Lisa arrives. Another tie to Memphis:

10/05/17 AT 12:42 P.M.

Hello Lisa,

I hope this email finds you well. I'm the executive director of historic Elmwood Cemetery in Memphis, TN,
where nineteen children are buried who died while living with Georgia Tann. Recently we erected a beautiful
memorial stone in memory of the children resting in
Elmwood.

Do you ever come to Memphis, and if so, would you
be at all interested in a book reading/signing/selling
event here? Elmwood is a nonprofit organization that
provides support to the community of Memphis in
many ways, one of which is history-based learning opportunities.

I hope to hear from you.

Warm Regards,
Kim Bearden

Lisa's thoughts whirl as she accepts the invitation to speak
at Elmwood Cemetery, in the Lord's Chapel, just up the hill
from the plot memorializing nineteen of the children who died
under Tann's watch. Could this place—this sad yet holy
place—be where those who survived finally come together?

A possible reunion schedule shuffles and shifts, but the stories continue. A steady stream of TCHS adoptees and family
members show up at Lisa's appearances through late fall and
winter and into the harbinger days of spring. They carry yellowed letters and documents from old file folders, including

sales pitches, of a sort, written by Tann as she marketed "orphans" to prospective parents.

> Take him and try him for a month. If you find him satisfactory, we can pair him up with another, similar offering . . .

> . . . a lively two-year-old boy. We'll have to wait a couple weeks for you to meet him. The little fellow has suffered a bump to his cheek after a fall from the swing . . .

The contents of these carefully preserved files emphasize the realness of these children, these families, the longing to have their experiences substantiated. At a book festival near Atlanta, Georgia, an audience member asks Lisa why families didn't track down their kidnapped little ones and insist on taking them back. "There were so many reasons," Lisa explains. "With her political alliances in Memphis, Georgia Tann was almost untouchable. She preyed on single mothers, indigent families, poor people who didn't have the resources to fight her. She altered paperwork to make children harder to find and to make them suitable to fill orders, the way she thought of adoption transactions. Ages and birth histories were changed."

Lisa elaborates on some of the subterfuge: "Children of sharecroppers were portrayed instead as the offspring of intelligent, beautiful college girls who slipped up with a med-student boyfriend and couldn't keep the baby or died in a tragic car wreck. Jewish families who wanted to adopt babies of Jewish heritage got Jewish babies. The baby might have been a Tennessee Baptist dirt-poor farm kid one day, and the next, he or she was of educated, well-to-do Jewish descent."

As the Q&A ends, a woman in the audience raises her hand and tentatively half-stands as she speaks into the pass-around microphone: "I was one of the Jewish babies."

The room erupts in a collective gasp.

After the event, Lisa and the woman, Patricia Forster, talk for a few minutes. Patricia tells a brief version of her story. They exchange contact information, and Lisa carries the memory with her to a book event in Florida, where a woman named Amy tells of her parents adopting a five-year-old sister for her from TCHS. The child was delivered to the back door in a big black limousine, typical of Tann's style. The recollection remains vivid for Amy.

As spring arrives with its too-brief beauty, plans for Lisa's Arkansas tour fall into place. Overwhelmed, she talks herself out of the idea of a reunion. Then she's back in. Out again. *Your schedule is already packed. Overloaded, in fact. You need to prepare for this trip!*

Writers don't plan reunions.

This is too far out of your wheelhouse.

Let it go.

She's nervous about logistics—petrified, actually. She has another novel to write. And yet these true stories won't leave her alone. They're an unexpected real-life sequel to *Before We Were Yours* . . . and they matter. These stories pursue her. They keep arriving, in more emails. They erode her decision the way the Mississippi River eats away at sandbars and banks to let the water flow.

The final nudge comes in the form of emails from two more survivors—a woman who managed to attend her birth mother's funeral and finally saw people who looked like her and another woman, abandoned on the courthouse steps in small-town Tennessee, who recalls the orphanage and Tann herself. It's early March. Time is short until Lisa's June appearance in Memphis, the logical place for a reunion, if there is to be one.

It's now or never. She emails Connie:

3/7/18 AT 10:18 P.M.

Hi Connie,

The thought of bringing TCHS survivors together has been on my mind . . . One event stood out as a good possibility for gathering survivors. June 10th, I'll be doing a speaking event for the historic Elmwood Cemetery in Memphis.

I've already heard from two survivors who hope to come, but being as this event is in Memphis and tied to the history of TCHS, it makes sense as a time and place for a gathering of survivors, perhaps with something additional just for the survivors after the public event.

After you've had time to ponder this a bit, I'd love to know your thoughts.

> Warmly,
> Lisa

Connie does not need to ponder. In the wee hours, she replies.

3/8/18 AT 3:11 A.M.

I'm in and will do whatever you need to help!
> Connie

She's too excited to sleep. At 3:22, she adds:

More to follow! It's 3 a.m. here, but I wanted you to know how excited I am to participate, help organize, etc.!

The answers await Lisa when she makes it to her inbox the next day. She dashes off an email while packing for another book-tour trip:

Hi Connie,

Wonderful! Thank you for being a driving force behind this idea of a survivor's gathering. I think (and have known for a while) this is an important part of the story. The true stories are as varied and unique as the children were when they were taken to the TCHS receiving home and of course the effects of those stories carry down through generations of children, grandchildren and greats.

It will be a full-circle moment, to be sure.

Lisa

Lisa certainly hopes so, although her excitement is mixed with trepidation and a stomach-churning dose of skepticism.

Will TCHS adoptees, most now in their seventies and eighties, trust a group of strangers and be willing to engage with outsiders? Do they want to delve into memories, many of which are distressing or long submerged?

Far away in California, Connie believes they will.

That, like her, they *must*.

CHAPTER 2

IN THEIR OWN VOICES

"It is a joy to be able to 'reunite' you."

THE IDEA OF A REUNION HAS WINGS, JUST AS CONNIE HAS dreamed. As Lisa has hoped it would, but feared it might not. The long-distance introductions of a tiny core group of adoptees begin.

Fact has met fiction, and the real stories are compelling, bittersweet, intensely personal, *and* part of history. "You create these fictional people, and you send them out into the world," Lisa tells a book group. "And the craziest thing is they come back home, tugging real people by the hand with them."

She connects Connie of California with a small circle of other women, and she gets to know them more in depth herself. Skype chats, email exchanges, and FaceTime conversations ensue. She sends an update when the core group of survivors grows from three to four.

4/11/19 AT 8:39 P.M.

Core group, meet Janie!
Janie came to the main receiving home on Poplar at

3½ years old and has memories of being there. She's one of the few with memories of the place.

All of you reconnected with siblings and birth families later in life, so there are stories there, as well.

I'll leave you all to get to know each other.

Warmly,

Lisa

Excitement grows as the new member is welcomed. Women with no memory of the infamous orphanage gain what they never imagined: a generous person who describes the place where their worlds were altered forever. Friendships deepen. "I've embarked on another journey . . . one I'd imagined many times but thought might never become reality," Connie writes, moved by discovering that she and other TCHS survivors "share so many emotions: the sense of never fitting in, the need to achieve, the need to prove ourselves, the fear of being abandoned."

Plans chug along, but hiccups, including the lack of a clear number of guests, keep them from being finalized. Venues are investigated and a few hotel rooms are booked, although a central meeting location and the weekend's format remain hazy. A wrinkle arises in the form of a note from Kim, the executive director at Elmwood Cemetery. Lisa's Sunday event in June is full and has a waiting list. *Might Lisa consider a second talk?* Lisa agrees, happy to have another event that adoptees might attend. Updated and as-close-to-official-as-possible emails are sent to all TCHS adoptees and family members known to Lisa and the core group.

Before We Were Yours has been out ten months when Lisa writes in an email:

It is a joy to be able to "reunite" you.

While the schedule solidifies, Lisa and Connie busy them-selves planning a separate weekend event limited to adoptees and their families. They reserve the stately Memphis and Shelby County Room at the Benjamin L. Hooks Central Li-brary, which lies just down Poplar Avenue from the site of the turn-of-the-century mansion that housed Tann's Memphis Re-ceiving Home for children. The very mansion that adoptee Janie Brand describes via email and FaceTime to her new friends on the planning committee.

The library houses archives of historical information re-lated to Tann's tenure in the city's adoption market. Newspa-per clippings, photographs, information about court cases, and decades of TCHS advertising pamphlets bearing the cherublike faces of Tann's young so-called inventory are waiting to be pulled from dusty file cabinets for reunion at-tendees.

Just after the email invitations go out, a follow-up message from Kim at the cemetery presents a new conundrum. Tickets for the second Sunday afternoon book talk have sold out within twenty-four hours. It's terrific news. *But what do we do now?* Lisa and Connie wonder. Without room for reunion-goers, an-other speaking event with ample space is needed to round out the weekend. A mild form of panic hits Lisa. June is the season of weddings and graduations. It's also less than two months away. Will there be any place available?

And she can't shake another idea, a more complicated one.

If this gathering is actually happening, true-life stories will be shared. These pieces of history should not be left to fade after June comes and goes. The voices of these stalwart survi-vors should somehow be preserved. For decades, these women and men have carried a strange history, one their families often did not wish to speak of—one involving adoption, a taboo topic in earlier eras, and ties to an epic scandal that was front-page news when it broke in 1950.

Tann too often overshadowed the stories of the lives that unfolded in her wake. Even during the 1990s, when the opening of Tennessee's adoption records led to many birth-family reunions, the national television coverage gave Tann a starring role.

She was a powerful and even, to some, enthralling villain.

But she is definitely not the victor.

This reunion is for her victims, many of whom have felt pressure to remain quiet about their pasts. Family stresses, the salacious nature of the Georgia Tann scandal, the fears of hurting adoptive parents' feelings, and even just the worries over upsetting life as it is have silenced them over the years. These survivors deserve to be heard, and not just on this one weekend, but for the future. Their stories should be documented by someone who can ask questions not only with skill but with compassion.

The TCHS reunion project needs a documentarian, a gumshoe reporter.

Lisa knows who she wants: longtime friend, author, and veteran journalist Judy Christie.

Judy

JUDY CHRISTIE HERE. WHEN THE PHONE RINGS, I'M LOOKING forward to my regular long-distance lunch visit with good friend Lisa. She and I first connected through a book festival ten years ago. We have a lot in common. We have been writers since childhood, we're both married to amazing public school science teachers, and we're girls who grew up in families filled with brothers. We love to laugh and have fun.

We are also type A, usually busy, and committed to meeting deadlines. Give us a project to brainstorm and step aside. We throw out ideas with abandon. We are curious about what goes on around us, and most of all, we each want to tell meaningful stories in this fractured world of ours.

As a book columnist for a newspaper in Louisiana, I'd received an early copy of *Before We Were Yours* and told readers, two months before it was released, that this would be a book they'd hear a lot about. "Take note," I wrote in my *Shreveport Times* column in April 2017, "this may be the best book of the year. Every now and then a novel comes along that sweeps me off my reading feet. *Before We Were Yours*, by Lisa Wingate, is such a book."

The novel exposes a chilling piece of history that I knew nothing about. I grew up in the South, was the editor of a daily newspaper in West Tennessee, and married a Jackson, Tennessee, native. *How had I never heard of this?*

It's April 2018, a year almost to the day since my column about her novel ran. As we chat, I'm eating a baked sweet potato with extra butter. I drink my midday Diet Dr Pepper. Lisa nibbles on a few nuts and drinks water. We may have lots in common, but eating habits are not among them.

These occasional calls break up the solitude of writing, and today's conversation seems routine at first. We talk about her travels and what a year it has been. She mentions her efforts to redesign her website. I tell her about a screenplay I'm revising and a freelance piece for a magazine.

The call is winding down when Lisa pauses and seems to take a deep breath. She speaks a little hesitantly. This is not her usual tone, and I sit up straighter. She tells me for the first time about the possible reunion and her worries about whether it'll come off all right.

"I think it's an incredibly cool idea," I tell her. She fills me in on her thoughts so far, and I jot down a few notes, a habit I've had since I was a teenager.

The location in Memphis seems ideal to me. So many stories began there. Georgia Tann's babies and children came mostly from Tennessee, although many were sent to adoptive families in California, New York, and other states. Lisa kicked off her *Before We Were Yours* book release tour in Memphis. Then she asks me an intriguing question, one she seems to choke on a little bit: "Would you, by any chance, be interested in being part of this? Possibly doing interviews and documenting the stories? These people have such incredible histories, Judy. These need to be written down, and if they're not, they are going to be lost."

My heart pounds. This is the kind of assignment that uses my journalistic background, my love of storytelling, and my interest in meeting fascinating people. Documenting these lives would be an honor. It would take me to Tennessee, a state filled with my kinfolks. Maybe Lisa and I will even help justice be served by giving adoptees the last word. *Take that, Georgia Tann.*

My usual practice of sleeping on important requests flies out the window faster than my intention not to grab a cookie for dessert. *I'm in.* My planner's mind runs through my calendar. "What's the timetable?"

"The reunion would be in June."

"Of *this* year?" Something lodges in my throat. I'm not sure if it's panic or sweet potato. Dates for events like this are set years in advance. Lisa is talking six weeks away. What about booking plane tickets? And a block of rooms? Is there any way to pull together a group of people from all over the country that quickly? What will attendees do at the gathering: *Hear about the novel? Tell their stories? Try to find more information about their heritage?*

Lisa fills me in on the details of their fledgling plans, the struggle to arrange venues, and the work of the core group of TCHS adoptees, busy coming up with suggestions for the shape their gathering might take.

It's all somewhere between set in stone and completely tenuous.

Bringing together people whose lives intersected in one place, more than a half century ago, but who have never actu-

This photo of Tann's orphanage on Poplar Avenue in Memphis was used in a TCHS brochure. Some say the building burned; others say it was torn down. Thankfully, it no longer exists.

ally met one another is, at best, a challenge. At worst, it could be a disaster.

Can it really be done? And in six weeks?

I stare at my calendar. Calculate. Plan. Pray.

Before the day is done, I have reorganized my schedule, blocked out a trip to Memphis, and committed to this event with all my heart. If there *is* a reunion, I will be there. And I will write the stories of all who want to share them.

It is late April.

In early June, we will be Memphis-bound.

We have no idea who else will be there. Perhaps there will be only four or five of us visiting in a hotel room. That will be just fine, I tell myself. Whoever needs to show up, will.

For now, my gathering of stories begins.

I order a half dozen of my favorite notebooks and two dozen Pilot Varsity blue-ink fountain pens.

PART TWO

RSVP

I can speak to you on the telephone ... I would
love an opportunity to honor my mother's story.

—EMAIL FROM AN ADOPTEE'S DAUGHTER
WHO CAN'T MAKE THE REUNION

WISH WE COULD
BE THERE

———

Raised as sociable Southerners, Lisa and I have hosted our share of events. Lisa was a pro at all-star birthday bashes for rough-and-tumble sons and puts together epic holiday potlucks. As for me, I've planned a surprise bowling party for my sister-in-law's sixtieth, an old friend's wedding reception at my house, an annual gathering of buddies who met in our college dorm in the mid-1970s, even the annual newsroom New Year's Eve party, back in the old days when people still smoked indoors.

Invariably, a moment of terror arises after the invitations are out of my hands . . . and beyond my control. I second-guess myself, start a few lists, and resist (or not) the urge to throw a quilt over my head.

This reunion, such a tender and unknowable occasion, raises similar—and yet new—questions. Lisa and I take several planning roller-coaster rides a week.

It's okay, we tell ourselves. If we host it, they will come.

Won't they?

Responses trickle in—a mix of "wouldn't miss it" and "so sorry I can't make it." We celebrate RSVPs from Connie, our planner and cheerleader, and three other adoptees who plan to attend. At least six of us will be there. Those who can't come send heartfelt replies with their reasons: a long-planned vacation to Hawaii, a grandchild's wedding, lack of money for an expensive plane ticket, a couple of surgeries.

The regrets contain another message, though—these kind people are devoted to telling their family stories and would be happy to visit long-distance. Perhaps life will bring us together down the road, maybe even at another reunion, but till then, I can capture their stories. I tear the plastic shrink wrap from my optimistic stack of new notebooks and begin to call the adoptees and family members who want to talk.

And I begin gathering pieces of history.

CHAPTER 3

A CADILLAC AND
A SECRET

————

"I know I have a mother out there somewhere."

ANNA WEST IS IN TROUBLE. SHE IS UNWED, PREGNANT, AND living in a boardinghouse on Walnut Street in Johnson City, Tennessee. Joseph, the father of the baby, is older by a decade or more and lives in a nearby town.

A tall, stylish young lady of nineteen, Anna gives birth at the boardinghouse on a cold February day in 1943.

The baby girl is beautiful like her mother, with blond hair and dark brown eyes. As newborns go, she is a stunner. Anna names the child Josephine, after the father. He is the one who pays the doctor and hospital bills, and his last name is used on the birth certificate. Anna's last name is the same as his on the document, and she is listed as his wife.

But as much as the new mother wants it to be, this is not true.

Joseph is already married and has a family. Anna tells her landlady, who is pressuring her for rent money, that he has sued his wife for a divorce and will marry Anna as soon as he can take care of the legalities. He visits the newborn baby, but then six weeks go by when he doesn't come back or send any money.

Anna is growing desperate.

Sandra

SANDRA MORRIS, A RETIRED EDUCATOR, GOES OUT TO LUNCH with a group of longtime friends once a month. The women have a glass of wine and discuss books. *Before We Were Yours* ends up on the book-choice list and grabs Sandra's attention. She knows her mother was adopted in Tennessee. Could this be her story?

After she reads the novel, she begins to ponder the documents she scarcely looked at after her mother died. Should she dig through her mother's papers to see if there's anything there?

She heads to the metal filing cabinets in the spare room and finds details she never knew, including the typewritten Tennessee Children's Home Society "Story Sheet" with dozens of heartbreaking details about her mother. Overcome with emotion, and eager to honor her mother's memory, she writes Lisa to share the story.

Months later, she hears about the planned gathering of adoptees and their families and wants to attend—but she has already booked a vacation during that time. Still, she feels drawn to this event and hopes to share her mother's story, so she and I connect over the phone. "Talk about fate," she says. "I was so fascinated and horrified by *Before We Were Yours* at the same time . . . My gracious. This is totally real . . . Except for the documents I needed to close out her estate, I really paid only cursory attention to the papers until I read Lisa's book."

She mails me copies of the documents so that I might understand the story, then help it live on. "What's exciting to me is that someone is going to hear my mother's story," she says. "This is a way for me to say, 'Mama, I love you.'"

———

ANNA RETURNS TO WORK JUST WEEKS AFTER HER BABY IS BORN. She has no choice after support from the baby's father dries up. It's work or be turned out on the street. She makes arrangements to leave baby Josephine at the boardinghouse with the owner, Mrs. Feathers, and goes to work, putting in long hours at a cafeteria and at a café. But on a waitress's salary, she can't keep up.

The TCHS Story Sheet notes explain what happens next, a tale that is harrowing and hard to digest. By June, four months after Josephine's birth, Anna has fallen behind on her room rent. She pays a little now and then but is getting deeper in debt all the time.

Still, she holds on to her daughter, even though it is an outlandish notion to those observing her plight. *An unmarried woman with a child? It simply is not done. This beautiful baby should go to a "good" home with well-off parents.* Adding to the pathos of Anna's situation is her sorrow over the death of her own mother shortly before she came to East Tennessee. Her father has remarried, and her stepmother, she feels, does not like her. Anna is adrift with a baby and no financial or emotional support.

Mrs. Feathers is losing patience. She complains to a juvenile judge about the late payments. The judge is unsympathetic to the single mother and criticizes Anna's second job as being at "one of our questionable cafés."

At the boardinghouse, an ominous cloud gathers over baby Josephine. *She's landed on Georgia Tann's radar.* Adoption workers keep track of the baby girl and write regular reports that sound like sales pitches for a new product in development. "A very fine baby," the paperwork raves about Josephine's looks. Mrs. Feathers is instructed to "keep the baby there." TCHS will pay until the child can be brought into custody. A doctor concurs that Josephine is "a prize baby."

TCHS workers investigate Anna's character, making notes. They attack her in their reports, using assumptions and insinuations. "None of it has been verified but some of it is true," a TCHS worker's notes read.

A removal case is well in the making. Even after being made aware of it, Anna will not agree to go to court to give up her child. She hangs on, works hard, clings to her little girl.

Her efforts do little good. A TCHS employee decrees, "If the mother refuses to appear in Court, I would commit the baby for adoption as an abandoned and neglected child."

It is now October, and Josephine is eight months old. Mrs. Feathers insists that she cannot keep the child any longer without adequate compensation and reports that Anna does not see the child enough. Besides, she says, the rent is fifty dollars in arrears.

Baby Josephine is only days away from losing her mother.

ELMER AND EVELYN PETERS are Pennsylvania natives, but they are on the road performing throughout the South in a traveling gospel show.

Evelyn badly wants a baby and learns that there is a way to adopt in Tennessee. She's heard that it might help if you are *from* Tennessee. Of course, a stable lifestyle would help, too.

She and Elmer settle in Knoxville.

He becomes the sales manager for a company that furnishes drapery, pictures, and objects of fine art to churches, theaters, and well-appointed homes. Besides owning an interest in the company, he makes two thousand dollars a month—a whopping thirty thousand dollars per month in modern-day dollars. In addition, Evelyn has plenty of family money.

When they apply to TCHS for a child, their financial means catch the attention of the orphanage's officials.

A pretty little girl soon becomes available, removed, allegedly, from an unfit mother and taken to the nursery at St. Mary's Hospital in Knoxville. Temporarily, she is called by the alias Priscilla in medical paperwork. The doctor thoroughly checks her out and assures TCHS that she is "a lovely baby but badly spoiled. She is very unhappy in the nursery."

Three weeks after being taken from her mother, Josephine lands in the waiting arms of Evelyn and Elmer. The child, not quite nine months old, is given the new name Helen, after the town where Evelyn was reared. The adoption worker offers glowing statements about the new parents: "Josephine was theirs from the minute they saw her. They were both overcome. To them it was just as sacred as though she had been born to them."

The adoption agency cannot hold back their praise for how wealthy and wonderful Evelyn and Elmer are. A sampling from a poorly typed report:

> Worker has known them and had interviews on the subject of their interest to adopt a child. They are both ideal parents—they would never see a child without being interested in whether poorly dressed or clad in finery. They just love children . . .

Elmer tells the worker that the new family is "ideally and completely happy."

The worker agrees: "Worker has seldom seen so complete preparation for a baby, everything is useful and beautiful . . .

Many of their friends have spoken to the worker in the interest of a child for this home." When she visits the home again, she says, "The baby has exquisite clothes. Many are handmade by relatives." And:

> They are a most charming couple and have a host of friends in Knoxville. They have not bought a home in Knoxville since they might find it advantageous to transfer to another section of the country in the development of their company.

Baby Helen. "She has been deluged with lovely gifts, including several war bonds . . . a prize baby," read an orphanage report following Helen's adoption.

As soon as the transaction is final, Evelyn and Elmer do indeed move away from Tennessee, heading to Pennsylvania, where Elmer works as an electrical engineer. But Evelyn's carefully constructed outline for life with a new daughter does not go as planned. With the adoption now official, the closely held secret of baby Helen's background festers. "I think that my grandmother wanted a baby so badly . . . she then wanted to hide anything to do with it," Helen's daughter, Sandra, says. The new father does not feel the same need for secrecy, however. Strife rips through the marriage.

Hiding the adoption wears on the couple, and Elmer leaves. "I think it just destroyed their marriage," Sandra says. "It was the biggest secret in the world. It was a subject not open for discussion."

Her parents do not tell Helen she is adopted until she is a teenager, when they break the news with the gift to her of a brand-new Cadillac. Helen becomes resentful and confused. She feels that Elmer has cut her out of his life, and her relationship with Evelyn is tense.

Her adoptive mother eventually marries the other preacher from the gospel show, and conflict grows between mother and daughter as Helen moves into adulthood. "My mother felt like she was supposed to be grateful that she was adopted," Sandra remembers. "The feeling I got was that my grandmother thought my mother wasn't appreciative enough."

Like many TCHS adoptees, Helen has no siblings. "All the time she talked about how much she hated being an only child," Sandra says. *I've been alone my whole life*, she would say.

Helen marries four times, has three children. She becomes a registered nurse when Sandra is a youngster, losing herself in her career, including helping with medical care for women in prison. "She worked. She worked, worked, worked," Sandra says.

Her mother's legacy of pain carries on with Sandra, who, as she grows, tries to earn family love that she feels she can never quite get. She lives with her grandmother, Evelyn, off and on, and they have a good relationship, but it, too, is tinged with the struggle for affection.

When Evelyn dies, she leaves a substantial amount of money to her adoptive daughter. The money, though, is not what Helen craves. She needs truth. In her late forties, in 1992, Helen can stand the secret of her birth no longer. She consults a lawyer to find out how to get access to her records, still sealed in Tennessee. "I know I have a mother out there somewhere," she says. "I want my mother."

When the records arrive, the anguish continues. She receives meager information about her mother but nothing about her biological father. "A search for your birth father is not being initiated, since there is no verification in the record of his acknowledging paternity," the state of Tennessee tells her. Despite documents that show Joseph as her father, she feels she has been rejected all over again.

Anger and hurt surge through her. Helen writes back, seeking clarification of these discrepancies. Her birth certificate says her parents were married, and she needs to know the details. "After all this time it just seems cruel that I can't know facts and information regarding my own history," she argues. "Could you please also tell me what actual leads, records, addresses, etc., you pursued in searching for my birth mother . . . If you know of any other ways that I can get my records opened up to me or whom I can ask for help, I will be eternally grateful." Her plea yields no additional information.

When Tennessee's records are officially opened a few years later, Helen pens a note on a pretty piece of paper. The message echoes that of many TCHS adoptees: "After waiting 52 years, I can now finally request by law that which was mine—my birthright."

A return letter hints at the besieged atmosphere within the

Tennessee Department of Human Services, where employees are dealing with a scandal they must now resolve, decades after it occurred. To a hurting adoptee, the delay is a fresh injustice. The state's answer stings. "The requests will be processed in the order in which they are received. We will advise you when we are prepared to do this."

Six months later, Helen receives another letter that says she must pay one hundred fifty dollars to determine her eligibility for the service. That is, she must *prove again* that she is a TCHS adoptee and pay for her information. There is a fee of fifty dollars for each additional record that is opened. And to add insult to injury, in addition to the fee, there will be a charge of twenty-five cents per page for copying.

She pays the money and waits. Another month passes, then two. Finally, Helen's sealed records arrive. An enclosed message strikes a more compassionate tone:

> Having access to your adoption records will evoke many emotions for you. Should you wish to talk with others who may have experienced similar feelings, you may wish to know about Adoption Support Groups across the state who can be a resource to you.

But as Helen reads the records, she does not see a desperate unwed mother. She feels instead a surge of hurt that her birth mother did not find a way to keep her. Until the end of her life, at age sixty-five, Helen remains angry about what happened to her as a baby. "I really believe that when she was taken away—from the time my mom stopped seeing her birth mom," her daughter Sandra says, "it imprinted on her and absolutely injured her, and it scarred her for life. She passed that on to her kids."

When Sandra digs through Helen's paperwork after reading *Before We Were Yours*, she discovers a letter written by her mother. The words are heartbreaking—"I now, after fifty-five years of being alive, finally know who my parents are." Although she learned their names, she never tried to locate them. She died bitter that they had let her go.

With no answers about what happened to Anna or Joseph, the questions that remain are now the burden of a third generation, eager to search for resolutions to worries about health and biology. "I started thinking, man, I'd really love to know about my mother's family's health," Sandra says. "I wish I knew who I took after." The hunt for relatives is compelling. "After so many years," she remarks, "I'd grown used to the fact that I had no family other than my sisters."

Sandra is continuing the search her mother put a halt to. She has delved into newspaper files and used Ancestry.com. She is chasing leads and finding scraps of information here and there. She believes that Anna, her biological grandmother, never married and died at age sixty. Sandra searches for those who knew her or who might have been related by blood. "I'm not going to give it up," Sandra says. "I'm going to keep at it."

She does this in honor of her mother and wishes she could offer her some final words: "Oh, Mama, you're loved. You were always loved."

IN BLACK AND WHITE

*S*andra's story of her mother's adoption, of her grandmother's tragic separation from her little girl, is hard for me to hear and impossible for me to set aside. It's heartbreaking to see in black and white, in the old typewritten documents, a life discussed in clinical terms, a child assigned value because of her looks, because of her marketability. And the desperation of a single mother—that's hard, too.

I add Helen's tale to our growing research stack. Starting with an empty backpack, I have begun to amass documents and old photos. I am already coming to dread the sight of correspondence signed in Tann's unmistakable spidery script. Her letters are typed on cute stationery featuring drawings of children, but they strike an ominous tone. The combination makes my stomach churn.

Some people say that boxes of papers were burned as soon as Tann died, that others desperate to hide their complicity in her crimes got rid of whatever information they could. Some still hint that adoptee records remain stored in Tennessee attics. People don't know what to do with them but can't quite bear to destroy them. Maybe they'll surface one day.

Lisa and I hope so. So many families are still out there, asking questions those documents might answer.

Each day I can spend only so much time poring over the records adoptees have sent to me, trying to make out faded type, looking at that spidery signature in letter after letter, imagining what parents on each side of the adoption were feeling. I pick up another file and begin to ponder the story ahead.

It is not my eyes that bother me, as I read these papers.

It is my heart.

CHAPTER 4

CLUES FROM
A HIGH SCHOOL
SCIENCE CLASS

"We've been expecting this call for years."

NORA RUTH MILLER IS AN OHIO SCHOOLTEACHER AND PASTOR'S daughter who picks up and moves to Michigan during World War II to help the war effort by working at an ammunition plant.

The adventure suits her lively spirit but goes in a direction she has not planned. She is twenty-six when she gets pregnant by the plant manager, who is in his forties.

He does not want to marry her. She does not want to marry him.

So Nora goes back home to Ohio and tells her mother and an aunt. Everybody agrees that Nora's preacher father does not need to know. The stigma placed on out-of-wedlock babies is gigantic, society's judgments harsh. It's one of several realities that feed Georgia Tann's adoption machine.

Nora is sent to Memphis to stay with her aunt, the mother of a one-year-old, until the birth of the baby. The story they tell others—including Nora's dad—is that she is going to Tennessee to help with her aunt's child.

For the last couple of months of her pregnancy, Nora lives in a home for unwed mothers, and she gives birth to a daughter on April 18, 1944. She does not want to give up the baby, but she knows of no way of keeping her.

The infant is sent to Georgia Tann's Receiving Home in Memphis, then taken to Nashville and kept at the TCHS home there for several weeks. The reason TCHS gives for moving the baby from Memphis is that a child cannot be put up for adoption in the city where she is born. Yet this is inconsistent with Tann's usual practices. Children born in Memphis are routinely kept there after adoption. The reason Nora's baby is sent to Nashville will remain forever a mystery.

Not far away, the Nelsons, eager adoptive parents, receive the message they've been waiting for. Their daughter has been delivered to the Nashville orphanage. Housewife Louise and accountant Doyle are ecstatic, but they are not allowed to pick her up right away. Instead, Louise is permitted to visit the infant for six weeks at the orphanage.

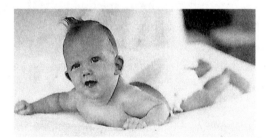

Diane is born in Memphis but moved to an orphanage in Nashville. Her adoptive mother comes to visit her there until she can be taken home.

Then the baby, whom they name Linda Diane, moves to her new home.

Where her adoptive parents are keeping another secret.

But all secrets have a way of surfacing, eventually.

Diane

"MY PARENTS NEVER TOLD ME I WAS ADOPTED."

Those words come from Linda Diane Page, age seventy-four when we speak.

Diane, who shed the *Linda* in high school because she had too many classmates with the name, won't be with us in Memphis, so she tells me her story in a conversation filled with startling details. Although she speaks with the intellect of the retired engineer she is, I hear a chord of melancholy in her words.

"I think my birth mother never saw me," she says. "She thought if she saw me, she wouldn't be able to give me up ... She wanted to keep me, but she didn't want to marry my father. She didn't see any way to keep me without marrying."

The book club at the Christian church Diane attends in Nashville has chosen Lisa's book *Before We Were Yours* for an upcoming discussion. "A couple of my good friends in that book club know my whole story," she says. However, Diane is not sure how she feels about discussing it with the group.

"I've never tried to keep it from anyone ... I don't deny it, but I don't go around telling it." She hesitates. "My adoptive parents gave me a good life. I was a spoiled brat. I went to dancing lessons and had the prettiest clothes and went to Vanderbilt."

When her name appeared on a short list of adoptees passed along to me by one of the reunion planners, I got in touch, explained our effort to document TCHS stories, and pledged not to intrude if she did not want to be interviewed. It took her a few days to get back to me. First, she checked with her daughters. "When you emailed me, I talked to all three of them because I knew it would affect them, too," she says.

Their response surprised her. They, like her, are interested in knowing more about the background behind her history. Behind *their* history.

SECRETS HOVER IN DIANE's young mind as she grows up, mysteries waiting to be figured out. Something's off, though she doesn't know what.

At puberty, she decides that maybe she is not Louise and Doyle's child but their grandchild, because they are so much older than the parents of her peers. "I thought that for a while . . . I felt like I had been watching a movie but could only see the center of the screen. There was so much more going on that I didn't see."

At about age fifteen, she makes her discovery in a high school biology class in Nashville, when she realizes that because she and her parents don't share certain genetic traits she cannot be their biological daughter. The age of her parents continues to provoke her curiosity, too. Her parents are always vague about how old they are. In general, they are friends with her friends' grandparents. "I was raised an only child. My parents were older," she says.

She has an idea that something is intentionally being hidden, because of her mother's reticence to speak of certain topics. "There was some inkling . . . things my mother wouldn't talk to me about." Her curiosity leads her into an argument with her mother. "I had a baby book," she recalls. "I never paid much attention to it." But she does now. "I knew my birth certificate was in there, so I went to look at it." Then she confronts her mother. "Have you ever been to Memphis?"

"No, I've never been to Memphis."

"Why does my birth certificate say I was born in Memphis?"

Her mother shuts her down.

As Diane's adoptive mother gets older, her health wanes, which raises questions about Diane's family medical history. Now married and with children, Diane has a daughter with emerging health issues, and she has questions. She needs answers. Growing up, she was close to four of her second cousins. She puts her long-held question to the mother of one of them. *Am I adopted?*

The woman hedges. "As far as I know, you're not adopted."

But a cousin, in his forties, comes to Diane with the truth: "I've always known you were adopted. My family promised not to tell."

An adoptive aunt and uncle lived near the orphanage in Nashville, and their children often played with children at the home. "My aunt and uncle knew about this," Diane says, recounting details of the secrets. "My older cousin told me that my mother and grandmother came there to visit me in the orphanage several times and brought clothes that my mother made for me. Then I was released to them when I was a couple months old."

Her adoptive father, Doyle, who lied about his age in order to help facilitate Diane's adoption, has died by the time she learns that she is adopted. "Everybody said Daddy wanted to tell me," she recounts. "I told my mother, 'I wish you had let me know.'"

"I didn't want you to think that there was anything wrong with you and that somebody gave you up," her mother, Louise, explains. In the days of Tann, that is a common answer from loving adoptive mothers who want the adoption never to be mentioned, of mothers who are well aware of the shadow that hovers over adoption in this era and want to pretend that the baby is theirs, or of mothers afraid that their child will choose the other mother if the truth comes out.

Diane's adoptive father, shown here, wants to tell her she is adopted, but her new mother resists.

Diane does not like the secrets. She gets on the waiting list for the Tennessee records in the 1990s; only it takes months. "When Tennessee opened the records," she says, "I got in line. I had my turn. I wanted them as soon as I could get them. What I really wanted to know was any genetic material."

Among the details she finds is that her birth mother, Nora, married a couple of years after Diane's birth but was unable to have more children. Sadly, she died before Diane started searching for her, but she had been on a quest to find the daughter she had not wanted to give up. That fact brings a lighter note to Diane's voice. "She looked for me, according to my cousin," Diane says.

Later, Diane meets her great-aunt, Zelda, with whom her mother lived while she was pregnant. "Tennessee gave me birth information, and I just got on the Internet and started looking.

I called and said, 'I don't want to cause any trouble, but you have a niece, Nora, right? I think she might be my mother.'"

Zelda, close to eighty at the time, responded right away. "We've been expecting this call for years."

With evident affection for her great-aunt, Diane describes the encounter: "We talked for a few minutes, but I knew it was a shock." Diane stayed in touch with Zelda and her husband, and Zelda mailed pictures of her birth mother. "They lived in Florida, and their daughter called, and they invited me down. My husband and I just got in the car and went. They are really nice people."

As with many TCHS adoptees, details of the meeting are still vivid years later. They met at a restaurant right off the interstate, and then the newfound relatives invited Diane and her husband to their home.

Not until Diane returned did she tell her children about the trip, and she eventually took, as she puts it, "all the family we had" to visit.

Now each of Diane's daughters has the desire to dig deeper. "The girls would like to find out more about my father, as to why my mother didn't like him . . . I doubt that anyone in his family knew I existed," she says. That, however, is a door she has not wanted to open.

Confirmation of her adoption, though, brought clues out into the open and helped Diane understand many things. One of her daughters, she says with a chuckle, marches to the beat of a different drummer than others in the family. Her personality always confounded Diane and her husband, also an engineer. "Who in the family is she like?" they would ask. "Where did she get those genes?"

Likely from Nora.

"Evidently my birth mother did what she wanted to do. And my daughter was glad to know there was someone like her. She was delighted to find out where it all came from."

In a sweet closing of the circle, her daughter names a child Nora. "I kind of liked the idea," Diane says.

They all would love to have known Nora.

But perhaps in the unique ways of mothers and daughters, of names handed down, and independent streaks, and the courage to march to different drummers, they already do and always will.

WHAT'S IN A NAME

*O*ne of my favorite questions to ask people in interviews is how they got their names. Names carry power, love, a glimpse into history—and almost always a story.

In my family, Ross is a popular name. It comes not from some lofty forefather but is in honor of a hired hand on my grandparents' farm on a dirt road in Arkansas. Ross. The middle name of my father, my oldest brother, his son, a first cousin, and his son. I even gave that name to the hero in one of my novels.

My name would have been Grace, but my mother married a Pace . . . and she didn't think the rhyme would do me any favors. Instead, my seven-year-old brother named me Judy Ann, which immediately dates me to the 1940s or 1950s. To this day, I ask, Who lets a seven-year-old name their child?

Lisa's parents argued over her name. "I was almost Stacia and called Stacy," she says. "It feels completely different. What would life be like with that name?"

One of the saddest things in getting to know adoptees is how each of them was given a name at birth—sometimes a treasured family name—and then renamed when they were adopted. One Memphis judge argued that they be allowed to keep their given names—but Georgia Tann prevailed. New names made it harder to trace adoptions and perpetuated the idea that the child had no past.

How tender it is that Diane's granddaughter Nora carries the name of her long-lost great-grandmother. The name honors her. Remembers her.

With the reunion three weeks away, I'm eager to hear the stories of the names I've only seen in emails. Something special is bubbling up here.

CHAPTER 5

IT'S ALL IN THE DNA

"At first I thought it was probably a mistake."

A YOUNG WOMAN WHO CALLS HERSELF VERA MAE BRINGS an infant into a pharmacy in a small town in West Tennessee. She tells the pharmacist she can't afford to keep the baby and wonders if he knows anyone who wants it. The child's name is John Stephen.

In a nearby town, Dorothy and Bill Gibson yearn for a baby. Somehow—the details remain unclear—they connect with the desperate young woman who is offering the unthinkable. Perhaps Dorothy and Bill are in the pharmacy that day and hear the offer themselves. Perhaps the pharmacist knows of their plight and contacts them with the news that they can become parents, almost instantly, if they'll hurry over.

They pick up their new son and rename him Glenn. His date of birth is listed as September 4, 1934, although no one knows exactly how old he is when he is offered up to anyone in the market for a baby.

Ten years later, Vera Mae, overdue to give birth, makes an uncomfortable seventy-mile trip to the Tennessee Children's Home Society in Memphis for prenatal care. It's clear that her plans for this baby go beyond those she made for little John Stephen. This baby will not be handed off in a drugstore.

On April 17, 1944, four days after Vera Mae arrives in Memphis, Theresa Celeste is born at St. Joseph's, a Catholic hospital that no longer exists today. Only four days later, the tiny Tennessee newborn is headed to an out-of-state home with the blessing of TCHS, escorted by one of Georgia Tann's colleagues.

The new parents, Sarah and Carl Kipling, living in New York City, have an inside connection with the orphanage, as many TCHS adoptive parents do. Carl's mother, a nursery school teacher in Alabama, is friends with a social worker at TCHS. She tells them about Georgia Tann, who is known to circumvent rules in the placement of children . . . for the right price.

In a letter of application to Tann, Sarah asks for a healthy baby of sturdy stock. She also acknowledges a potential problem: "You will note that we are of different faiths, but this has had no effect on our happiness. We are prepared to give a child the proper religious training, in the Jewish faith because that is my religion, and my husband is in accord on the subject. However, the child's previous religious background doesn't concern us at all."

It doesn't concern TCHS, either. The orphanage happily accepts a thousand dollars—equivalent to about fourteen thousand dollars today—in exchange for Theresa Celeste. Tann writes the Kiplings about "our procedure in placing children in other states" and explains that "the child will be placed in your home on a probationary basis for the first year, during which time she may be returned if not entirely satisfactory." Tann lies and tells Sarah and Carl that the infant's birth mother is a young girl who can't keep the baby. The reality is that the mother is in her late thirties with four children at home and three already given up for adoption. The couple, like so many TCHS adoptive parents, knows none of this. They are over the moon about their sweet new daughter, whom they rename Bess Ellen. They gush with tender joy at their good fortune.

"We are very anxious to adopt an infant baby girl in good health."

—LETTER FROM BESS'S ADOPTIVE MOTHER TO GEORGIA TANN, DECEMBER 11, 1943

But their family is now part of a tangled secret that will keep brothers and sisters apart for decades.

WHEN THE WOMAN WHO called herself Vera Mae—her real name is Elsie Clara—hands over her infant son in a drugstore, she begins a pattern of giving up children. A total of four children will eventually be put up for adoption, and the next three, after John Stephen, all go to Georgia Tann at TCHS: a daughter, born in 1938; another son, born in 1940; and finally, Theresa Celeste, in 1944. These four full brothers and sisters are dispersed throughout the country. Three half brothers and a half sister remain with Elsie Clara. An infant sibling dies. The family farms for a living, but they are very poor.

Four children given up.

Four children kept.

The children who were adopted will later question whether the family made a business of selling babies to Tann.

Perhaps when Elsie Clara first walked into that pharmacy and announced that she had a baby to hand off, she popped up on Tann's radar. Was John Stephen the first of her babies that TCHS caught wind of? Was the family put on Tann's watch list? Or was Elsie Clara offered a deal, a bargain struck for the purchase of future children? Whatever the mother's motivation may have been, a family of siblings is separated.

It will take a near miracle, with an assist from DNA and a determined teenager, to bring them back together.

Bess

WHEN I CONNECT WITH BESS WINTERS, SEVENTY-FOUR AT THE time, the adoptee reunion planning is under way. She wants to come to Memphis, where so much damage was done to her family. But as a retired licensed practical nurse living in upstate New York, she watches her budget and cannot afford the trip. She is eager, though, to talk about her years-long passionate struggle to find a sister and two brothers.

Despite having lived a privileged life in her adoptive home, her childhood filled with Broadway plays, a trip to Cuba before Castro came into power, a visit to California, a train trip through the Rocky Mountains—"We went everywhere," she says—she would have traded all of that for her siblings. "I would have given my right arm to live with my brothers and sisters."

"Everyone exclaims over her sunny disposition
and her ready smile . . . I am sure it is not only
her parents' prejudice when I say that she is a
remarkable child . . . May we thank you again
for the happiness you have been instrumental
in giving us."

—LETTER FROM BESS'S ADOPTIVE MOTHER
TO GEORGIA TANN, OCTOBER 24, 1944

Hers is a captivating tale of triumph against what seems like the greatest of odds. And it is a reminder of how Tann and TCHS affected not only the adoptees but generations to come. "I just feel that this woman Georgia Tann committed so many crimes," Bess says when we chat on the phone.

She is charming and intense and speaks of her birth siblings with excitement and love, their connection a rare blessing at this stage of life. "I have all my paperwork out," she tells me.

Days later, a manila envelope stuffed with her information arrives in my mailbox. It is full of not only photocopies but also original documents. As I slowly remove each piece from the large packet, I feel humbled by her trust—and saddened by what I read. Letters from her adoptive mother to Tann. An adoption decree. An ad Bess once placed in a Nashville newspaper, trying to find her siblings.

The ad never produced any leads. Years would go by before clues would come in a different way. Bess's siblings, doled out one by one at Tann's whim, will remain separated for almost a lifetime until TCHS records are opened. Then there is still one more brother they do not know about.

Chills run down my arms as she shares the story in a long telephone visit. She read *Before We Were Yours*, and the picture on the cover reminded her of herself and her sister. When the sisters get together in the novel, she says, "it was like Lisa was writing about our family, too. Georgia Tann . . . she was a terrible person. She separated families."

As a child, of course Bess has no way of knowing the strange path her family journey will take. Its beginning is preserved in the large envelope of documents she mails to me. Letters from Tann are included, often with instructions—such as to send Tann one hundred forty-eight dollars to cover transportation and travel expenses to prepare for Bess's placement. "Please make check to Miss Georgia Tann and mark it 'Transportation,'" Tann writes in 1944. The amount would be about twenty-two hundred dollars today.

Bess's new mother, Sarah, like many other adoptive mothers, writes Tann regularly, lengthy letters in elegant handwriting. Her delight in her baby daughter rises from the pages like a pleasing perfume. "She is considered beautiful by everyone so that we feel that we aren't too prejudiced. Again, thank you for her. We surely do love her and will be good to her."

However, Sarah's correspondence also prods for legal documents, a vein of anxiety and suspicion underlying her communications to Tann. "We have never received any legal papers consummating her adoption—are they essential? If so, should we take any steps that we haven't taken?"

Another letter gives insight into the trauma of World War II, coupled with the need for a mother to know more about the child she has adopted. The letter opens with thanks for "our wonderful baby. She is so sweet and good; we are certainly very fortunate." It shifts then to news of a house call from their pediatrician and asks for information for the doctor about tests done at birth.

> I would appreciate greatly if you would send the information for him. Then, too, if you could send some proof of her birth or some papers concerning her, so that I can get her a ration book. It is impossible to get one at my local board without a birth certificate, hospital record or something to prove that she is here and is mine. Her evaporated milk requires red points, and when she gets vegetables I'll need the blue ones.

Tann responds with the needed information, and Sarah promptly writes back: "I have already procured her ration books." When Tann receives that letter, she scrawls on the bottom of the page, to an unknown office worker: "Please acknowledge and tell them I'm out of city on vacation but to please let us here [sic] from baby."

The reassurances about a Jewish upbringing for Bess,

spelled out in that other note from Sarah to Tann, do not come to fruition. The couple, not particularly religious, celebrates Christian and Jewish holidays, and Bess becomes a Catholic as a young adult.

But Tann has much bigger concerns than religious preferences. In December 1944, she contacts the Kiplings and tells them she anticipates changes in Tennessee's adoption laws. "We feel it might be advisable for those who have children in their homes not yet adopted to complete these adoptions at an early date," she writes.

She goes on to say that, of course, they should do so only if they "are fully satisfied that the baby you now have in your home is the one for you." The plan to finalize the adoption can be carried out by a TCHS worker, who will travel to New York, Tann says, because the Tennessee court understands "this war emergency and difficult time of traveling with children." Then Tann requests $160.68, about $2,300 today, for expenses, with the check made out to her personally and marked "For transportation and court costs." The Kiplings work with Tann to finalize the adoption, never going to Tennessee or to court in New York.

Bess is only five or six when she asks her mother if she was adopted. "I was a curious child. All my cousins had black hair," she says.

"No," her mother tells her.

She persists and asks if her mother is *sure*—because, she points out, she doesn't look like anyone else in the family.

Her mother capitulates: "Yes, you were adopted."

Bess becomes terribly upset, so her mother backpedals and says she was just teasing: "No, you weren't adopted."

The conversation illustrates the confusion of Bess's upbringing, a life filled with many material blessings but also laced with secrets and unanswered questions. She will not learn parts of the truth until she is in her thirties, and she will be middle-aged before she encounters other surprising pieces of information. "I did," Bess tells me, "have a sense that something was . . . I don't know what you'd call it . . ." Her voice trails off.

She and her parents live in New York City until Bess is six, then move to their second home, an eighty-five-acre farm in White Plains with a cottage and a main house, a beautiful albeit remote and sometimes isolating place for a little girl. "We had a lake, and I had horses," she relates. "It was happy, but it was lonely." So she makes up siblings. "I had two dolls. One was a boy and one was a girl. I used to pretend they were my brother and sister."

Though Bess doesn't know she is adopted, she is aware that she was born in Memphis, and her inquisitiveness grows as she grows. "Why were you in Tennessee?"

"We were just passing through."

And that is that . . . until Bess is thirty-eight years old and an odd family drama unfolds. "I got a letter in the mail from the Department of Vital Statistics about my adoption," she says. *The adoption that her mother had denied to her.* Her adoptive parents are long since divorced at that point, and her father has remarried. Without her permission, Bess explains, an older family member wrote to the state of Tennessee claiming to be Bess and asking for information; hence the surprise letter in Bess's mailbox. "When I got that letter, it was such a shock. I had lived a lie. I wasn't who I thought I was."

She confronts her parents. Her father is apologetic. Her mother is upset.

"My mother said she couldn't face the fact that she didn't give birth to me." Bess remembers being told that her adoptive father had had the mumps and could not have children. The scenes that take place are familiar to other TCHS adoptees who lived with a sense of something not being quite right and with mothers who so badly wanted the child to be theirs and no one else's. Bess is quite close to her aunt, her mother's sister, but this woman, too, has kept the secret. When the truth comes out, the aunt insists to Bess's adoptive mother, "I told you that you should have told her."

Bess doesn't hold the secrecy against her aunt, but it still hurts. "The first couple of months, it affected me emotionally. I was sad. I was questioning. My aunts and uncles *knew*."

Does she still resent the collective silence? "Oh, no, no, no, no." She went to therapy and worked through it. "I didn't hold it against my mother, either. It doesn't matter. It's over. I just hold it against Georgia Tann . . ."

However, with this news, the secrets of Bess's birth are just beginning to be exposed. "I knew I was born in Tennessee, and my heart was always down there. I always thought about Tennessee . . . I always thought I was a Southerner. It was a very strange thing, my affinity for Tennessee," she says.

When she begins to dig into her biological roots, she consoles her adoptive mother by telling her, "I'm not looking for a mother. I'm looking for my sister." Her search is tedious and frustrating. Her birth mother used a variety of names on the adoption paperwork. In convoluted family records, her name is sometimes Valeria, and the last names vary. "It's all mixed up," Bess says.

Her birth father, Thomas, was forty-four and had two boys from a previous marriage, and he and Elsie Clara lived together in a small town in West Tennessee. Thomas was a hard worker. "They stayed there. They got married after giving away babies." *Or*—the question lingers—*were they selling them?*

When Bess starts looking for her family, Tennessee's adoption laws have not yet been changed. The records are sealed. Bess writes the state of Tennessee and finally finds a judge who will open her file. In the papers, she discovers the names of one biological brother and sister and learns more about her history. Methodical about her quest, she joins the ALMA Society, a nonprofit organization that helps people connect with their birth families. She writes down every step she takes and keeps a large file of letters. "I searched counties," she says. "I knew they were out there because they were in my papers."

Then she makes a discovery.

An older brother named Jim.

"I screamed across the street, 'I found my brother!'" she says. "I located him in Arizona and called him on his birthday. He was home sick with a cold. He was very happy . . . I think he was stunned."

Before she and Jim meet, Bess tracks down her sister, Susan, in Nashville, by calling the sister's adoptive mother. "She said, 'I can't believe it! She's always wanted a sister.'" Susan's adoptive mother instantly dubs Bess her *second daughter*. Again Bess rushes outside. She tells me, "When I found her, I screamed, 'I found my sister!'"

An activist for open adoption records, Bess writes a letter to the editor of her local newspaper and contacts the governor's office. "I finally was able to find my biological family," she says. "Thank God it wasn't New York, because I couldn't get any information." Her words during our interview come faster and with more heat: "I wanted the state to know that it's not a bad thing to have an open state for records. Once you reach a certain age, I think you should be able to have your records open."

Bess's three daughters chip in for a trip to Tennessee to reunite her with her sister, Susan.

"We got on a plane, and we flew down to Nashville," her

daughter Emily says. "We're not big spenders, but when it's something important like this, we find the money."

The first meeting in the Nashville airport is as full of emotion and drama as any movie scene. Bess, thirty-eight at the time, wears a shirt that says I FOUND MY SISTER. Susan, forty-two, has a shirt that says HERE I AM. "It was like we were walking in slow motion, and no one else was around," Bess says. "We went into each other's arms. I didn't hear a thing except I heard her whisper, 'I love you.' She and I are exactly alike." The two sisters ultimately find their biological mother, through a reluctant half sister living in Tennessee. "She really wasn't that welcoming," Bess admits.

When they meet for a larger reunion, her birth family says they did not know that anything was going on with other children. No one remembers Elsie Clara being pregnant. The reluctant half sister, who was sixteen when Bess was born, doesn't say anything when they first arrive at her house.

But she does something curious. She immediately walks across the room and checks a strange little bump of cartilage on Bess's ear, an identifying mark since birth. *Had she known all these years that she had a little sister?*

Their birth mother is elderly and is suffering from dementia by the time they visit. "I really didn't feel anything. To me, she was just a lady sitting in a rocking chair," Bess says. "I *had* a mother. I was sort of angry that we didn't get to know each other. It was very strange."

Susan, who was placed for adoption at three weeks old, is more emotional during the visit.

"We're your grown-up babies," Bess says, trying to connect to the woman in the chair.

For a sad moment, Elsie Clara seems to come out of her fog.

"Oh, my babies," she moans. "I used to line up five little chairs in a row."

That is all the emotion they will get from her.

At a gas station in rural Tennessee, Bess also meets a half brother, who was married and had a child by the time she was born. "He got out of his car, and tears were streaming down his face."

"I knew you were out there, but I didn't have any way to find you," he tells her.

A lovable character, he has since died, but Bess tells me an animated story about a pig roast he hosted the second time she and Susan visited. Her voice is full of amusement and tenderness when she says, "She and I slept in the same bed, like we were kids."

At breakfast the morning after the pig roast, everyone teased one another. "You joke around like you're kids," a family member said.

The family welcomed her with love. "They are wonderful, wonderful people. They're wonderful," she says. Then sadness enters Bess's voice. She and her sister stay in touch, though finances keep them from visiting often. "She needs me now, but I can't afford to go to her . . . She's like part of my heart. It would have been wonderful if we had known each other all these years."

Jim

ON THE DAY OF THE BOLT-FROM-THE-BLUE CALL FROM BESS, Jim Andrews is forty years old, the same age his parents were when they adopted him. Bess happens to reach him because he is down with a nasty bug and taking only his second sick day in twenty years.

Now retired in Arkansas, he recalls that moment: " 'I'm your sister,' a woman said. I thought it was a joke."

Born on March 1, 1940, he considers himself one of the lucky ones, adoptees who went to good homes. Like several men I interviewed, he is not all that interested in talking about the past. "When Bess called, I didn't know if I wanted to meet her," he admits.

But in Washington, D.C., on business, he decides to fly to New York to see her. "That was a fiasco," he says. News cameras show up, and he is rattled and steps into a restroom to compose himself. "That wasn't what I wanted."

Despite that, their meeting turns into a nice occasion, including time with one of Bess's daughters, Jim's new niece. A short time later, he happens to be in Nashville on Thanksgiving and has dinner with Bess and their sister, Susan. "We had a nice visit," Jim says. The women tell him they want to go see their birth mother, who lives a couple of hours away. "No, no, no. I don't want any part of that," he says. He has never gone to the town where his birth mother lived, and he has no interest in doing so now.

Adopted by wonderful people, Alice and Morris Andrews, a dentist and his wife living in northern Mississippi, Jim eventually learns that his birth certificate is totally false, with no information about his birth parents. His adoptive father was a relative of Tann's, and his story is typical Tann. "She must have been a distant cousin," Jim speculates. "I don't know, but there is some distant family relationship there . . . My dad called up Georgia Tann and said, 'We're looking for a baby boy. When one comes through the door, give us a holler and we'll come to Memphis.' "

Jim as a toddler. "We think they were selling us to Georgia Tann," he says.

Although he is reticent to talk about his adoption, Jim is thankful. "I was extremely fortunate to be adopted by them," he says. "The Tennessee Children's Home Society was good to me."

At age eleven, he was told he was adopted. "It meant nothing to me. I just loved my family so much and had such a great family relationship. It didn't faze me."

Yet like nearly all adoptees, he had moments of wondering.

"Maybe as I got older, I'd be sitting in an airport and watching and wonder if I was related to someone walking by," he confides. But those were fleeting thoughts. "I never sat down and agonized about it." He wouldn't have thought of searching for family. "I knew it would hurt my mother ... My family is my mom and dad," he says. "The other people gave me away. They didn't want me."

And yet, after reading *Before We Were Yours*, he contacts Lisa, and during her Arkansas tour, he visits one of her book events to say hello and tells her a few details of his life.

A story of siblings lost and found begins to sort itself out . . . slowly.

Glenn
<hr />

THE BABY GIVEN AWAY AT A WEST TENNESSEE DRUGSTORE grows up lonely, an only child in Ohio with the Gibsons. Dorothy, a homemaker, and Bill, an American Baptist preacher, dote on him in their own way, although Bill is often gone.

Young Glenn. "Some of it we will never know . . . I just sit and cry that they had so many wasted years," says Glenn's daughter.

At some level, he knows that something about his life is . . . off.

He is sixteen and at his grandmother's funeral when he picks up a family Bible and flips through it. In the handwritten family history is a small notation.

Adopted.

He confronts his parents. "You were never supposed to see that," they say. "We are never going to talk about it."

Glenn is shocked, hurt, and confused. And more than a little angry. As their only child, he feels isolated and uncertain. He graduates from high school and joins the Air Force at the tail end of the Korean War. In the years that follow, he tries to ask his parents about his adoption, but neither of them is willing to tell him the story. The message he gets is *Please don't ask.*

Glenn marries the woman who has now been his wife for fifty-nine years, and from the beginning he talks to her about his hidden past. He spends thirty years in a good career as a time-study engineer for an International Harvester plant—and decades wondering, constantly wondering. Through his long marriage and long career and the raising of his own children, he is more than just curious about where he came from. He *needs* to know.

He has always longed for siblings.

His daughter, Victoria Watson, tries talking with her grand-mother about the adoption, but Dorothy will divulge nothing. "If she was going to tell anyone, she would have told me," Victoria says.

When Glenn's adoptive parents die, in the 1980s, he tells Victoria that if she wants to look for his family, she can. "We didn't know a ton," she says.

First, she tries the Internet. "I got absolutely nowhere," she recalls.

Then she writes the state of Tennessee and is excited when the piece of mail comes. It only produces more disappointment. "We didn't really get anywhere. We just thought, 'Oh, well, it wasn't meant to be.'"

Then a friend finds their own family members on Ancestry

.com, and Victoria is encouraged and mentions it to Glenn. "He was a little skeptical," she says. But she convinces him to try checking his DNA anyway. A woman who turns out to be Glenn's cousin responds, and Victoria finally has a name to follow.

The cousin is happy to connect with someone, and Victoria is talking with her when another first cousin match pops up on her computer, giving her goose bumps. "We had given up hope at this late date," she says.

By the time the mystery is completely solved, Glenn's wish will be granted in abundance. He has three full siblings and four half siblings.

But the final bits of the puzzle will be pieced together by an unlikely source.

Josh

BESS BRAGS WITH A GRANDMOTHER'S DELIGHT ABOUT HOW smart and well-rounded her grandson Josh is. Age eighteen when I catch up with him, Josh likes to play the guitar and the piano and to ride his dirt bike. He also enjoys doing things outdoors with Bess, who lives an hour away.

The pair's strong connection goes back to Josh's babyhood. When he and I connect for a phone interview, he describes his grandmother in warm terms: "She is friendly, has a great sense of humor, and makes people happy." In a sweet twist, the words are very close to those Bess's adoptive mother used when describing Bess in letters to Georgia Tann.

Family means everything to Bess, a trait she has passed on to Josh. Married once for fourteen years, she is long divorced and has three grown daughters, seven grandchildren, and two great-grandchildren.

When he is sixteen, Josh decides he wants to solve his family's mysteries. Interested in math and science, he asks for an Ancestry.com DNA kit for Christmas. "I really wanted to find out where all my ancestors came from," he says.

His mother, Bess's daughter Emily, waits until spring to order the kit. "He wanted it for Christmas," she says. "I kept pushing it off until it was on sale."

If she had only known.

"It came, and it was really simple," Josh tells me. "You just spit in a tube." A month or two later, he gets the results—including a match with a man in Ohio.

"At first I was like, That's probably a mistake." But then he gets a message through Ancestry.com from a woman who explains that the DNA match from Ohio is her father, an adoptee. "My dad doesn't know anyone in his family, basically," she tells him. "I'm looking for my father's birth family."

"Oh, wow," he replies. "My grandmother is looking for her brother."

The chills escalate.

The news excites Emily, a school secretary in her forties. "Right away I thought of my mom," she says. "Oh my gosh, there's someone out there." From childhood she has known that her mother, Bess, was adopted and felt she was missing something in her life. When Emily and her sisters squabbled as girls, Bess would say, "You should be happy you have sisters."

The woman who has emailed Josh is Glenn's daughter, Victoria. Within a couple of days, Bess reaches out to her, saying, "I think your father is my brother who I've been looking for, for over thirty-five years."

Victoria calls her father, cautious. She's tried to verify all the details before sharing this with him, to make sure everything is on a good path for her dad, whom she describes as "a very tender teddy bear kind of soul." And he is skeptical about the news. The ups and downs of searching and the longing in his heart have been hard on him.

"Dad," Victoria says, "this is DNA."

It takes him a while to process the revelation, and then he calls Bess, reassured now that she is his long-lost sister. "He had big tears in his eyes," Victoria recalls. "He couldn't believe he was actually speaking with her."

An outgoing woman, Bess is beyond delighted that life has brought her together with her brothers and a sister. Even before she knew about Glenn, Bess had wondered if there might be another sibling out there.

Now she knows.

During our interview, Josh takes time away from celebrating his eighteenth birthday to describe his interest in genealogy, which led to the discovery that has so enriched his grandmother's life. He chats happily about it as though he is talking about any of his other teen hobbies. An honors student, he is soon to be a freshman in college, where he'll pursue a premed course of study. The family is having a birthday barbecue, and his grandmother is on her way over. Nearly two years have passed since Josh found her brother for her. They have reunited, and in a matter of weeks, Josh will meet his great-uncle Glenn in person.

He is happy with how the DNA connection worked out. "That was really cool," he says. As for the effect of Bess's adoption on him, he's not concerned. "I've just thought of it like I'm a combination of everyone in my family."

Glenn sends Josh a collection of fine silver as a gesture of gratitude. "This is a token of my appreciation for you having your DNA put on Ancestry.com," he writes. "Without that I probably would never have found my brother and sisters."

Emily knows that something special happened with her son's detective work. "It's so weird, but there was something that kept telling Josh to do the DNA," she says. "Wow. Look what he did. He made a whole new story."

WHEN GLENN AND BESS finally reunite in person in Nashville, along with their sister, Susan, the moment is dramatic. They hug and weep and touch one another. They have much in common—they like to garden, love animals. They use a lot of the same phrases and have the same mannerisms. "Is it a coincidence or did they pick this up in utero?" Glenn's daughter wonders.

Bess is ecstatic. "Glenn walked in the door, and, oh my gosh, it was a wonderful, wonderful reunion. I said, 'Come here, you old buzzard.' I'd never said that to anyone. Then I pinched his cheek."

She soaks in the special words. *Brother. Sister.* "Those words . . . I always wanted to say, 'my brother, my sister.' It just felt so absolutely wonderful to say."

As they get to know one another, they long for all the years they missed. "It's happy and sad," Bess says. Her daughter Emily agrees: "I'm just thankful they're in my life now." Finding his siblings has put into place a missing part of Glenn's heart. The not knowing was awful. "It filled something for him," Victoria says.

He talks to his sisters on the phone, and they visit in person when they can. On a trip to Tennessee, the three travel to their birth-family home in a small community. A half sister and two half brothers have already passed on, but they are able to meet one of those half siblings' sons, their nephew.

"They're still cotton farmers," Victoria says. "We've met all of them."

The siblings are now spread from Arkansas to Ohio to New York to Tennessee, and Bess wishes they all lived closer to one another. Emotionally, though, they are remarkably tight, as if to make up for the lost years, their bond evident in how each one speaks of having these *new* siblings.

Reunions unfold over the years, but they have not yet had one big gathering. Brother Jim is not quite ready for that. He tells me he feels as though he might be disrespecting his adoptive parents if they have a big family reunion, although he is slowly reaching out to his siblings individually. After some hesitation, he and his wife make a trip to see Glenn and his family. The dining room table is beautifully set, and Victoria cooks a pot roast. They take pictures and talk about fishing. Both Jim and Glenn express pleasure about having met.

"I would have loved to have lived in a family of kids and been poor," Glenn says. Such is his affection for his siblings. "It would have been worth anything to be with them."

The thrill of his visit with Jim, on the heels of a trip to see his sister Bess, though, is almost too much for Glenn, who makes a trip to the emergency room the next day, worried that he is having a heart attack. All turns out well. Stress and fatigue—and pure happiness—from the stunning reunions apparently overwhelmed him.

Victoria, who calls me on the way to the hospital to see her father, rejoices that the brothers and sisters know one another now. "I believe it was a gift that God pulled off . . . My dad would like to see his siblings as much as possible before they pass," she says. "I just sit and cry that they had so many wasted years."

Young Josh, whose interest in DNA changed lives in a way he could not have imagined, encourages people to search for their relatives: "If they have any doubts about it, just go for it . . . You might just find someone."

TENACITY AND TIME

*P*iecing together stories of siblings who struggled for decades to find one another brings to my mind those movies where the hero absolutely, positively refuses to give up. A similarly heroic level of determination, I now realize, drives family member after family member as they seek out connections.

Through their words and their actions, they show that nothing is more important than family—and, just like in the movies, they know the clock is ticking.

These adoptees inspire me to mail a favorite book to my oldest brother, to spend a few extra days at home in Louisiana for the holidays, to make a goofy birthday video for my great-niece, and to text a cousin. *Don't put it off,* these voices warn me.

Adoptee Glenn, in his eighties, provides a visceral reminder of this lesson. When I first reach out to him, he is too sad to talk and asks his daughter, Victoria, to speak with me instead. His half brother Al, whom he had located only a few months before in a small town in Tennessee, has recently died. "It's kind of bittersweet for my dad," Victoria explains. "He's just found them, and then his brother dies. He's missed out on so many years of having siblings."

Her father made a hurried trip from Ohio for one last visit with Al, who was quite ill by the time Glenn arrived. They shared a tender goodbye.

Al looked at Glenn. "That's my brother?" he asked.

"Yes," Al's wife confirmed. "That is your brother."

Glenn moved closer to him. "We didn't get to play as children," he said, "but we can play in heaven."

He made it there in time for that one last conversation. One last promise. A little more time with someone he loved and a chance to say the things that mattered. So many of those who passed through Tann's hands never had that chance.

Glenn has precious memories because Victoria didn't give up. Because Bess wouldn't take no for an answer. Because young Josh was curious. And each one acted out of love.

Lessons worth carrying in our hearts.

Lessons I feel like I'll be hearing more about in the days ahead.

CHAPTER 6

ONE DAY OLD AND
SENT TO MEMPHIS

"My wife is the one who found my birth family."

HATTIE ESME ARROW IS FORTY YEARS OLD WHEN SHE TELLS her children she is going to Paris, Tennessee, to have an abdominal tumor removed. The truth is much more complicated. The cause of Hattie's weight gain and rounded middle has a life of its own.

A son arrives, the last of her eight children by three fathers. This baby, named Edward Jasper Adams, is born on the evening of February 29, 1948, in McSwain's Clinic in Paris, and the next day he is spirited off to the Tennessee Children's Home Society in Memphis, one hundred fifty miles away.

A week later he is adopted.

It is an oft-used method of procuring inventory for Georgia Tann: communication with a network of doctors and outlying clinics, so as to get her hands on newborns.

Hattie Esme signs the paperwork with a made-up name, Mary Adams. She claims in the records that the child's father, Gus Adams, died in 1947, and that the boy needs a home. However, the man listed as his father actually died nineteen months before the baby was born.

False names. False dates. A false history.

The baby's mother is a sharecropper, the records say, and overweight. "Birth mother feels she cannot keep the baby. She is now on relief. She is very average from a plain family of farmers."

She has a bad reputation around town, and her other children are treated poorly by local folks. "They're Hattie Arrow's kids," people say, as if that explains everything.

THE JOHNSTONS—CLARA, THIRTY, AND Bud, twenty-eight— live in Memphis. They have tried to adopt for several years and are thrilled by a sudden call from TCHS. They are invited to come pick out a child. They are given the choice of a boy or a girl.

They choose a boy. A son. Baby Edward, whose name becomes Michael.

The adoption moves him into a substantially better life.

His is a tale of six siblings who stay with their mother, one who dies as an infant, and just one who is adopted.

Michael will not know the rest of his story for more than fifty years.

Michael

MICHAEL JOHNSTON LIVES IN MEMPHIS, NOT FAR FROM WHERE our reunion is to take place. In one of those strange happenstances of adoptee connections, an adoptee who'll be joining us sends Michael's name my way. One story leads to another. Word gets around. With an estimated five thousand—and perhaps more—children having passed through Georgia Tann's system, they are out there everywhere.

When I phone Michael, age seventy at that point, he speaks with the enthusiasm of a busy man who is happy with his life. He tells me he is planning a trip to Nashville to see a brother with whom he has connected only in recent years. Eager to discuss his life story, he speaks with obvious love for his wife, Grace, and describes how she persisted in helping him find out his family history. We talk for a long time, and I make plans to speak with Grace when they return from their trip. The energy level is high, and I can tell that Michael feels he is living in the midst of a miracle.

His information has come to him in bits and pieces. "The forms were full of lies," he says. The record of his placement shows a Memphis address, but even that appears incorrect. He does know this, though: "April 8, 1948, that was the day my parents picked me up." The only fee listed on any of the paperwork is a $2.50 charge for an adoption change of name. Michael surmises that his adoptive father's oldest brother, who had money, paid for his adoption. "He had a very instrumental part

Toddler Michael. He believes an uncle who had money helped finance his TCHS adoption. "I was lucky," Michael says. "I was only eight days old when I was adopted."

in my being adopted. At the time, they didn't know about the gruesome goings-on at the Tennessee Children's Home."

From his earliest days, Michael knows he is adopted, thanks to a book on the subject that his parents own. "I would sit on their laps, and they would read it to me . . . I couldn't have asked for a better upbringing," he says. He is raised in Memphis, only about a half mile from Elvis's home. He tells the anecdote cheerfully: "We'd go over, and I'd get autographs from him and sell them to my cousins from out of town."

His adoptive father, Bud, is in the Navy in World War II and afterward goes to work for the railroad, where he and Michael's uncle work for decades. Michael follows in the family tradition. Before his career is established, though, he spends two years in the Army in Vietnam. "Uncle Sam sent me a letter," he recalls, his voice dry. "Your local draft board wants to see you." He was three credit hours from being a senior in college.

A man of strong religious faith, Michael is brought up Baptist, his father a deacon in their church. "I grew up in a good Christian home, but I also grew up an only child," he says. The comment is reminiscent of those of other adoptees who, though in happy homes, tell me they mourned the absence of siblings. He turns to his faith as he discusses how he found his family: "God let us do this in the right time."

For years, he is not that interested in looking into his past, but Grace wants to know more about his medical history. Each has been married once before, and now they have been married to each other for thirty-six years. When Michael develops vascular issues, they send a letter to the Tennessee Department of Human Services and receive a letter saying that the records can be opened for one hundred fifty dollars, plus twenty-five cents a page for copies. "I was still humdrum about it when my wife started. It took months to prove I was who I said I was . . . it was kind of an ordeal for me to get my adoption records," he says.

When he does, only four siblings are listed. Swept along with Grace's efforts, he is hooked and remembers the exact dates of important discoveries in his search. A major anniversary is June 17, 2005, when he receives his paperwork from the state. Grace immediately attempts to run down the surname Adams. The lies begin to surface. "Georgia Tann wasn't terribly concerned about records," Michael says. "We had exhausted everything in West Tennessee and could find no trace of this Adams family. My wife just kept pushing." With Michael's health issues, Grace wants to know about medical information that should be shared with his sons. Plus, Michael is close to Grace's brother and sister, and she believes he deserves to know if he has living siblings of his own.

Grace gets on the computer every afternoon and on weekends. "I would look up the name Adams and hit dead end after dead end," she says. "I thought, 'There's got to be another way.'" Among the meager clues she has to work with are the names of Michael's birth mother's brothers and sisters and the name of a town in Michigan.

Grace remembers a landmark day: "One Saturday, when I'd done everything I could on the computer and nothing was matching up, I called directory assistance in Michigan." After she explains that she is trying to locate her husband's family, the operator comes up with one possible number.

When Grace calls the number, she gets a recording. "I put a message on her answering machine: 'Ma'am, I'm sorry to bother you. There's a possibility you may be related to my husband . . . I understand in this day and age if you don't want to call me back.'"

Improbably, she has found a cousin who lives in a house that belonged to the cousin's grandparents, dead for years . . . and the phone number is still listed in the cousin's father's name. The woman calls back immediately, asking, "What makes you think I'm related to your husband?"

Grace gives her some background, including a list of names.

"Let me call you back. I need to make a phone call," the stranger says. She hangs up, calls Michael's birth sister, then calls Grace back. "I'm your husband's first cousin," she admits. Michael arrives home from work just then. "Wait just a minute," Grace tells her.

"I handed the phone to him. From that point on, there's been a family relationship."

Michael still remembers that date, too: October 29, 2005. "I didn't find my family until then. My wife is the one who found my birth family."

His older sister Mildred calls soon after the cousin, saying, "I understand you're my brother." She goes on to inform him of the lie her mother told about the tumor. "It all makes sense now . . . You've got a brother and a sister. I don't know how they're going to take this."

Barely two minutes into the conversation, Mildred asks if she can ask him a personal question.

"After what you just heard from me, you're entitled to ask me anything," he says wryly.

"Michael, do you believe in the Lord Jesus Christ as your personal Savior?" He tells her "yes" and learns that his siblings are devout Christians, a bond that unites them to this day.

MILDRED'S YOUNGER SISTER MARTHA recalls quite well the "Are you sitting down?" moment when she first heard about Michael, and she recounts the conversation to me with delight.

Mildred calls her on that very same Saturday, saying, "You're not going to believe this. We have another brother. I just talked to him, and his name is Michael. Call him if you want to."

"Nah, I'm going to wait." Martha's uncertainty is evident. "I'll get with him later."

The next morning, she feels antsy . . . as if she has to do something, but she doesn't know what. So she calls her pastor for guidance. After church on Sunday night, she decides: "I'm going to try to call this Michael guy."

She and her baby brother talk for an hour and a half, and a special relationship takes root. As they get acquainted, their conversations range from big topics, such as what life was like with Michael's birth mother, Hattie Esme, to their mutual dislike of milk. "He will not drink milk, and I haven't drank milk since I quit the bottle," Martha, seventy-four when we visit, tells me.

Before they wrap up the call, she tosses him a typical sister taunt:

"You definitely grew up with a better life than we did . . . The only thing you missed out on was brothers and sisters—and that's not always all it's cracked up to be. You've got yours coming, little brother. I took it all those years, being the youngest, and now you're the youngest."

Michael does not hesitate: "Bring it on."

That their mother kept this secret from them, not even disclosing it right before she died, at age fifty-eight, baffles the siblings. An aunt confesses, "Well, she didn't take it to the grave. *I* knew."

The family secret wasn't so secret after all. Michael's biological grandmother also knew. She saw a photo taken of him when he was born and said he looked like Granddaddy. And Michael's oldest half brother, sixteen when Michael was born, spoke of a brother on his deathbed. "We've got another brother," he whispered, troubled in his final days. The family soothed him, thinking he was delirious and remembering a brother who died as an infant. He insisted: "No, we've got another brother."

"He might have known," Martha says. "He might have suspected. Mother might have told him. He never breathed a word. She never talked about it."

Although Michael has gained two sisters and a brother, he does not get to meet his other siblings, the sisters who died in 1995 and 2002 and the brother who died in 2001, plus the brother who died as an infant. But as Martha tells me the story from her perspective, she reels off those he *has* seen with the practice of a family matriarch. "He's met our niece's daughter, our great-niece; and he has met one of my sister Sandy's children, and he also met my sister Audra's grandchild, and her ex-daughter-in-law." And that is just a start.

During his initial telephone visits, Michael learns that both his sisters live in Arkansas. Mildred tells him, "You're family. You're coming to stay with us." Three weeks later, Michael and Grace join them for Thanksgiving dinner.

Thanksgiving that year takes on a whole new meaning. In addition to a big meal, they feast on meetings with other kinfolks, family stories, and lots of sibling teasing. Pure gratitude is the sauce that covers everything.

Michael's wife recalls the day: "There was a close bond. They accepted him, and he accepted them . . . I was just overjoyed. He was developing a relationship with his family like I'd had with mine all along. To me it was as if they'd only been apart for a few months, not for more than fifty years."

Though many lies were told, one thing is true: Michael's adoption saved him from struggling through the sort of unhappy childhood his siblings endured. While the orphanage paperwork is not flattering to Hattie, her reviews from her grown children are worse. Even as older adults, they're still upset with their mother. Martha tells about each of them suffering frequent beatings, including with a wooden two-by-four. "She couldn't take care of another child. She never took care of us."

Michael is sad but grateful. "None of my siblings have anything good to say about our mama," he says. "I was so blessed to grow up in the family I did."

The birth-family resemblance is strong, though, and his sisters love telling him how much he looks like his older brother Sammy, who initially is reluctant to meet him. Sister Martha recalls the first time she saw Michael that Thanksgiving holiday. "I was looking out the window, and I saw him getting out of the car, and I said to my husband, 'Oh my God, he looks so much like Sammy.' . . . I opened the door. It was like we had been together before." Michael and Martha wonder if they share the same birth father, but they have not tested their DNA.

As soon as Michael and Grace come inside and meet Martha, she phones her daughters to tell them that her brother is there and that he is a nice person. "Meet your uncle Michael," she says with a big smile when they arrive.

There is another round of calls a few minutes later, this time with Michael bringing in his son Kurt. "I want you to talk to your aunt," he says, and hands over the phone.

Kurt informs his newly introduced aunt, "I can tell Dad is excited. He gets this funny little laugh when he's excited."

On Friday after that first Thanksgiving, they jump right into what Southern families do: they sit down together and share stories. But they also look at TCHS adoption records. "I saw the handwriting on there and knew it was Mother's handwriting," Martha says. At that point, the paperwork is moot. "I was sure by then that he was my brother."

Michael's voice is emotional as he recalls that first meeting and how his wife's determination made it happen. "She forced me into finding my family," he says. "It's been a real blessing."

Martha

BORN MAY 22, 1944, IN WEST TENNESSEE, MARTHA IS FOUR when her mother tells her she is going away to have a tumor removed. "I remember her going to the hospital and having surgery. I remember they brought her home in an ambulance, and I remember they carried her in the house. That's about all I remember."

Martha's world with her birth mother is a sad contrast to the one Michael will experience with his adoptive parents. She grows up not knowing about Michael, but she does know that something is different about her family. Her parents have a child born with spina bifida. He lives five weeks and dies in June. In August, Martha's dad passes away. She is only two.

"I don't remember any of that. I knew I had a dad and didn't understand why he had died," she says.

The stigma of her father's death, her mother's behavior, and poverty all hang over the children. People are cruel. Martha remembers being in town and going into a store to get a five-cent ice cream with a brother and a sister. The children are about ten, eight, and six. "We were in there having ice cream, and someone started talking to us, a man. And he said, 'Who's y'all's daddy?' Someone said, 'Those kids don't have no daddy.'"

An older half brother becomes her father figure. "Growing up without a father was difficult, but I didn't know it until I was in school," she says. "People would say bad things . . ." Hattie and her six children live in a small, four-room house with a tin roof. "We lived out in the country on the farm . . . my family was very poor," Martha says. Her late father had not even been a sharecropper but was merely a farmhand.

Our lengthy phone conversation has been filled with lots of emotion, and Martha pauses to express a moment of compassion for her mother. Her voice wavers as she says, "She was in her thirties when my dad died. She had needs and wants. She was still a young woman, and she was caring for six kids. She did a lot of yelling. She always seemed bitter. Maybe that was because Daddy died and left her six kids to raise. I know it was a hard life . . . She had been nothing but a homemaker." During those hard years, Hattie Esme never feels good, has high blood pressure, and is anemic. Every morning she cooks breakfast on a wood stove, then puts great northern beans in the pot, boils potatoes, and makes cornbread while the stove is hot.

Martha's thoughts are darker when it comes to Michael's probable birth father, a married man who might be her biological father, too. "I never liked him . . . I remember him being around our house too much," she says. Again, she feels for her mom, though: "I know mothers will do whatever they have to for their children."

The man's visits are seared into her memory. "Sometimes in the summer, when I was about eight, I'd put a quilt on the floor to sleep in the living room . . . There was only one fan, and we'd sleep with the door open. I can remember hearing him come in at night and get in bed with her. I knew it wasn't right for him to come into the house at night."

This upbringing is hard on her, and Martha will seek a better, more stable life. Her best friend's boyfriend is in the Air Force with a guy named Raymond, who complains that he does not get any mail. "I started writing to him," Martha remembers, "not even thinking anything would come of it." Raymond visits her for five or six days when he's on leave in October 1961, they continue writing, and he returns at Christmas and asks her to marry him.

She graduates from high school in 1962 and marries in November of that same year, not having seen him for a year. The Cuban Missile Crisis has roiled the nation, and he cannot leave his post in Kansas. Martha travels to Kansas on her own. "I got there on a Saturday, and we got married on Thanksgiving. We have two wonderful daughters and five grandkids and two great-grandkids."

They have been married for fifty-three years when Raymond falls terminally ill. Michael enters their lives in time to get to know his brother-in-law and to help out as Raymond's health fails. Reuniting with a lost sibling lessens Martha's sadness and brings new joy to her life. "You're the best thing that's happened to my wife in a long time," Raymond tells Michael. "I know if something happens to me, you'll be there for her."

"You want me to call Uncle Michael?" Martha's daughter asks one time when Raymond's health declines. They know he will drop everything and come. All they have to do is ask.

Michael is also good for Raymond, giving him a new reason to do things. Since it is hard for Raymond to travel, Michael and Grace go with him and Martha on trips, including a driving tour to Canada for a grandchild's wedding. "All of my grandchildren love Michael, and my girls just love him," Martha says.

In 2009, Martha and Michael travel together to visit an aunt—the one who helped Grace connect by phone with Michael's sisters. "We took off and went to Michigan," Martha says. "We had such a good time, and we talked. We laughed. We probably cried."

The cousin, cognizant of how time is moving on, jokes about

the get-together. "It's good we're finding relatives, since we're losing so many," she says.

When Martha's beloved Raymond is rushed to the hospital shortly before his death, she calls Michael, who lives nearly two hundred miles away, in Memphis. "I'm on my way," he says.

He is happy to make all the trips. "I told Grace I just couldn't get peace," he says. "I really feel like I need to go be with my sister."

After Raymond's death, Michael and Grace continue to visit regularly. "To me, now and even right after I met him, I felt like he'd always been there," Martha says. She sometimes dreams that she is young and that Michael, an adult, is there. "I had several bad experiences as a teen," she says. "Now I think about Michael. He's there and protects me . . . I feel like we've gotten so close that sometimes it's hard for me to realize we didn't grow up together."

She has kept her promise to make him pay as the baby of the family. "I love to tease him, and he loves to tease me. We have such a good time together . . . I pick on him a lot, and he picks on me a lot." Martha calls Michael "the tumor" and "the furry-faced baboon." But their primary endearment for each other: "You wrinkled-up fart."

Even though Michael and Martha and their older sister Mildred, now in weakening health, bonded quickly, their Midwestern big brother, Sammy, was skeptical of the newfound sibling and remained standoffish for a year or so. Then, in 2006, a cousin set up a family reunion for everyone to meet Michael. "We drove to Michigan to meet all of them," Grace says.

Sammy said he was tired and didn't want to go. His wife persuaded him.

The meeting surprised each of them. "I see my brother in a Bob Evans parking lot in South Bend, Indiana," Michael says with a touch of bemusement. "That's my brother right there. I see a family resemblance."

Sammy's wife gasps to her husband, "My God, that's you ten years ago."

At the same moment, Grace tells Michael, "That's what you're going to look like in ten years."

"There are so many things that parallel in our lives," Michael says. A decade older than Michael, Sammy had also been in the military. Instead of naming their oldest sons after themselves, making them a "junior," as is tradition, they each made their younger sons their namesake. They both started smoking at twenty and quit at sixty-three. They dress alike; when they meet, they are wearing the same tennis shoes, same types of shorts and shirts.

Adoptees and family members spend hours studying documents, photographs, formal records, and handwritten notes, seeking clues to family histories.

Now that they see each other more, Grace says, "We'll get to the motel, and the guys have the same color shirts on." "We've never known anyone with the name Kira," Michael says. Yet his brother has a great-granddaughter Kira, and Michael has a granddaughter named Kira.

These days, with the brothers' relationship solidified, Grace and Michael and his brother and sister-in-law go to the Grand Ole Opry in Nashville each year. "We get together and play cards and just have a ball," Grace says.

"He and I have been as close as two brothers can be," Michael agrees. "We're best friends."

PART THREE

Reunion

To this day I search Ancestry.com and use my DNA to discover if there is some familial connection somewhere. If I could just learn the truth of my mother's story, I might find some peace.

—EMAIL FROM AN ADOPTEE'S CHILD

WHERE THE
STORY BEGINS

———

*A*s a cub reporter, I learned that every story starts with the old-fashioned who, what, when, where, why, and how. The 5 W's and 1 H, they're called in journalism school. The answers to those questions lead you, like a stone path into a garden, to the heart of any story, from the breaking-news account of a devastating tornado to a visit to the White House for lunch with Nancy Reagan to the splendor of a rocket launch from Cape Kennedy to a profile on an aging farmer who grinds his own meal and shares his cornbread recipe.

Those same questions serve me well as I get to know adoptees and family members with strong, unique voices. Preliminary phone calls lead to stories of agonizing separation and joyous comings-together and make me long to visit with each adoptee in person.

With the TCHS reunion a couple of weeks away, I consider heading to Tennessee early for a handful of road-trip interviews. Then, amid the ongoing scramble of planning, we receive the disappointing news that one member of our core group of adoptees may not be able to attend. Patricia Forster, "the Jewish baby" who caused such a stir at Lisa's book festival talk last fall, may not be up to the trip.

I fret—not only that this event could be a bust without folks like her, but that her memories might be lost. I need to sit with her. To listen. The urgency may seem melodramatic, but who knows what the future will bring?

A few decades ago, I started my career as a hard-news reporter. I know how to get places in a hurry. I don't want to miss this story. I cash in all my frequent-flier miles and get on a plane.

CHAPTER 7

BORN ON CHRISTMAS DAY

"I was one of the Jewish babies."

Born on christmas day in 1942, the little girl is a gift her mother decides not to keep. Left at a Nashville hospital by the parent she is never supposed to see again, she is called Carol by the doctor.

Thirteen months later, Georgia Tann comes up with a plan for little Christmas Carol.

Seven hundred miles away in Buffalo, New York, the Fromers have been married for twenty years but have failed to conceive a child. By now Howard, age forty-six, and Larisa, forty, are too old to adopt conventionally.

Larisa comes from the Lower East Side of New York City, raised in a tenement. She is born to Russian parents, new to the United States. Her twin sister dies at age eight from a tooth infection. The family is close, but Larisa's childhood is poverty-stricken. Her situation is not unlike those of the youngsters Tann targeted in the rural South. Larisa and the other neighborhood kids gather around a candy and ice cream store and vie for leftover fountain drinks, eager for a few sips of something sweet. Larisa, a tall girl, is happy when she gets the treats.

Howard's relatives are also immigrants—from Poland. By

age fourteen, he holds two jobs in Buffalo, delivering Western Union telegrams and working as a busboy at the original Statler Hotel. He uses his paychecks to buy galoshes, which he then sells on street corners when it snows. That enterprise, undertaken while he is still a teenager, propels him and a brother to start a vigorous retail shoe business in Buffalo; in the years to come, they will own seven shoe stores.

An uncle in New York City makes Howard's match with Larisa, setting his Jewish nephew up with a friend's Jewish daughter. Howard has a car and money that he doesn't spend, and Larisa is interested.

Until they go on a date to Niagara Falls, and Howard attempts to kiss her.

She promptly slaps him.

"But they told me all the New York City girls do that," he sputters.

Not Larisa.

In the weeks that follow, he persists in his courtship, writing letters and returning to New York City to see her. They marry in 1924, in her parents' tenement apartment, and head to Buffalo.

Larisa is an independent woman, ahead of her time in some ways. She wears pants and drives a car. She bowls and does good works at the temple. And she accepts the fact that there is not going to be a baby. Until 1944.

Her two sisters and two brothers' wives are all expecting children. Larisa desperately wants to be part of the group of new parents. Someone tells her about a doctor in New York City who knows something about a way to get a baby.

Larisa calls on the doctor, and he confirms the rumor. "I heard about a place down South, in Tennessee," he says, "A place where you can adopt babies. But it's expensive."

Howard, who grew up in a household with six brothers, is not keen on the idea. However, Larisa threatens to leave him if he does not try the Tennessee Children's Home Society. Whether she would have left is doubtful, but he adores her too much to risk it. Their quest for a baby is under way in a city and state they have never visited.

Although Howard gives in to getting a child from TCHS, his preferences are definite. He wants a boy who will follow him in his business—and no diapers. With the faraway aid of Tann, Larisa and Howard settle on a blond-haired, blue-eyed boy.

Two weeks before their son is to be delivered to them, though, a telegram arrives from the orphanage: "Boy no longer available. Have thirteen-month-old girl. Are you interested?"

Patricia

PATRICIA FORSTER, NOW AGE SEVENTY-FIVE, IS FLIPPING THROUGH a *People* magazine, awaiting her turn in a suburban Atlanta nail salon, when she stops, startled.

A short article rouses memories she does not often revisit. A new novel is out, based on the shocking true story of a Memphis orphanage.

Patricia's nails are scarcely dry as she heads across town to buy the book, *Before We Were Yours*. When she returns home, she eyes the novel with curiosity and a touch of apprehension, opens it, and is hooked. In addition to the plot, she is drawn to the story's images of dragonflies, symbols to her of transformation, clarity, and illumination. They remind her of her own life.

A few days later, she sees a notice that the author is coming to the area for a book talk. Once more she is caught off guard.

Is this coincidence or fate? She argues with herself about the event.

Do I want to go?

You read the book. Do you really need to go?

In the end, it is not so much that Patricia talks herself into attending. It is that she cannot talk herself out of it.

The day arrives, and she puts on one of the stylish, flowing outfits she prefers. Her son-in-law picks her up and drops her off at the book festival. A capacity crowd resurrects her doubts. Lisa is already onstage when Patricia tentatively snags a seat in the middle of the room.

As the presentation unfolds, the author relates the true story that inspired the fictional *Before We Were Yours*.

Patricia already knows some of the details.

Lisa explains how Georgia Tann played God with the lives of children through TCHS. Adoptees were often sent to older parents and presented as possessions to mold as desired, with little to no consideration given to how a child might fit into a family.

"'They are blank slates,'" Lisa quotes from Tann's repertoire of sales pitches. "'Ours are only the cream of the crop.'"

The children came with intricate histories frequently fabricated from Tann's imagination. Lisa mentions the non-Jewish babies being misrepresented to Jewish adoptive homes in the wake of the Holocaust.

Hands fly up as readers clamor to ask questions.

Patricia, with her dark hair and generous smile, is a gentle, unassuming person with the kind of lap that grandchildren happily climb onto. She's not one for speaking up in a crowd. She sits and listens.

"Any last-minute questions?" the moderator asks.

The session has almost ended.

What comes next surprises Patricia. "I don't know where I got the courage to do it, but I stood up and said, 'I was one of those Jewish babies.'"

Her quiet statement causes an unexpected hubbub. The woman next to her treats her like a celebrity, and Lisa's helper invites her to come forward for a photograph.

As the crowd disperses, Patricia heads to the book-signing table for the picture and to have her copy of *Before We Were Yours* autographed. Lisa is excited to visit with her, the first of the Jewish babies she has met.

"To a woman with a story to tell," Lisa writes on the title page of Patricia's book.

FOR PATRICIA, A NEW part of her story opens up with the novel and encounter. She has been mostly fine with leaving the past alone through the years. "I have always been the reluctant one about looking," she explains as we prepare to sit down for a morning interview several months after she heard Lisa speak. "I was blessed."

A mother and adoring grandmother, she has made peace with her family background. If she examines it more deeply, she thinks, she might find things she does not want to know. Things she does not need to know at this season of her life.

But now something compels her to tell her story to me.

And I am so pleased that I came to hear it. The last-minute flight and frequent-flier miles are well worth it as I conduct my first in-person interview with a TCHS adoptee.

A gracious woman, Patricia greets me in the lobby of her high-rise retirement apartment building pushing a wheeled cart for balance—too proud, she admits with spunk, to use a walker. A hodgepodge of bright art created by residents lines the lobby walls, and a receptionist at the counter smiles, her gaze curious as she ponders the reason for my visit with Patricia.

Our elevator chat is not that of strangers but of new friends. We have visited on the telephone and connected over shared experiences, including the deaths of our mothers when we were about the same age and our years in the South. As the former editor of a newspaper published near where Patricia was born, I am surprised that it took me so long to hear about the TCHS scandal. She finds it ironic that she wound up down in *Georgia*, a move South that she never would have expected but made to be near her daughters.

Stepping into her apartment is like entering a professionally staged antiques gallery. Each square foot is a delight, a tableau that tells a story, no detail left untended. I learn that the walls were painted to her specifications, the paint names carefully recorded and shared. The colors complement everything from the scarf she wears to an Art Deco piece of furniture that moved with her when she downsized, not long ago. She conducts a quick tour of her treasures and mementos.

She lingers on sentimental stories of family objects—an evening bag that belonged to her mother, a picture of her father. We wind up at a tiny table by a window, beautifully set for breakfast, the view one of a courtyard with a large tree Patricia loves. Always full of gratitude, she repeats her thankfulness for her new space here, for this particular apartment, for that tree, different and beautiful in all seasons.

Like life.

She serves breakfast with the polish of a hostess who has done this many times. Her appreciation of entertaining is clear, whether she's hosting the young grandson who loves to sleep over on the fold-out couch or her oldest, dearest friends from New York, her supportive posse.

With coffee and extra croissants, the conversation about her life catches fire, and I begin recording her story. Maybe it is age that compels Patricia to document her experience. Or family. Or a need to preserve it for history. Or the desire to ensure that something like this never happens again. Most likely, a combination of all four factors. "I don't have any secrets," she says as we begin talking in earnest. "It's all about what we do with what we were handed."

Patricia's smile is huge as she begins an oft-told family tale. No one knows what happened to the orphaned boy, past diaper age, who was to have been given to Larisa and Howard, but family recollections are clear on what happened after that: "That's how I entered their life." She speaks pragmatically, slipping into the third person. "That's how they got Patricia. They didn't get their boy. My aunt loved to tell this story."

Tann sends a purported nurse by train to Buffalo to deliver baby Carol, soon to be renamed Patricia. Overcome with excitement, Howard's whole family waits at home. They are gathered in the kitchen when the child arrives. The courier puts the girl on the floor with a warning: "She doesn't walk, but she can crawl, and she doesn't like to be held." The scene that follows goes down in the annals of Patricia's family record books. Aunts and uncles re-create the moment for years. "The woman put me on the floor, and I crawled over to my dad and pulled up on his pant leg. The way my Aunt Myra told it, he picked me up and didn't put me down until I was six years old."

Throughout those early years, the family would tease him: "Howard, she can walk."

"Why should she," he would reply, "when she has me?"

Tears sparkle in Patricia's eyes as she finishes telling this favorite story. Having talked for hours, we pause for lunch, letting the emotion settle for a while over another meal, which she again serves with the kindness that radiates from her. She digs deep to answer questions and shares dramatic stories from the heart. As she talks about all that happened, she returns to Larisa, the woman who became her adoptive mother. "I wish I could have this chat with my mom," she says.

Perhaps together she and Larisa could clear up some mysteries. Patricia's early life, it turns out, is based on extraordinary lies. Lies that will not be revealed for decades. Tann tells Larisa and Howard an elaborate yarn about their little girl's heritage, fiction full of details sure to please the Jewish couple. Her manufactured background is documented in TCHS records and goes like this:

> The baby's birth parents were young. Her father was a Jewish medical student. Her mother got sick and died after delivering the baby. The grandparents owned a haberdashery shop. "Son," they said, "you're too young, and we're just too old to take on a baby. This baby has to be put up for adoption."

The yarn climaxes with Tann's happy pronouncement to Patricia's enthusiastic new parents: "You have yourself a little Jewish girl."

Thus, a non-Jewish baby born on Christmas Day in Tennessee is raised by a Jewish family in New York.

Upbeat overall, Patricia looks wounded as she discusses the transaction: "Georgia Tann was a good saleswoman. She had good products . . . child trafficking. What a lowlife." The time leading up to baby Carol being put on that train and delivered to Howard's family gathering in the kitchen is, to this day, a troubling void for Patricia. She wonders where she was for the early months of her life. *Did the doctor send her to the Memphis orphanage? Was she in foster care? Rejected by some other adoptive family?*

"It remains a mystery," she says. "Where was I those thirteen months? It was a long time to be on the shelf in Georgia's business." What few hints she has about her earliest months are disturbing. She knows that she arrived in Buffalo with a big boil on her ear, wasn't used to being held, and wouldn't sleep.

That, thankfully, was before Larisa and Howard, who immediately devote themselves to their new daughter. They drive her around in their car to lull her to sleep and unceasingly shower her with love. "Clearly you were beautiful, but you were the saddest baby I had ever seen," her dad will later tell her, after she's grown. As a new father, he dedicates his life to erasing that sadness. The feelings that start when she crawls toward him will continue until his death at age ninety-five.

"He always called me 'Doll' and 'Dolly' and 'Dear Darling Daughter Patricia,'" she remembers with a mix of happiness and sorrow.

Adoption, however, will not be a topic for discussion in their home. She learns young to tread softly when it comes to talking about it with Larisa. "I'm not sure how old I was when I started asking about the other mother and father. My mother didn't talk about the adoption. She really wasn't open to ever discussing it. As far she was concerned, I was hers."

Once, when Patricia raises the subject, her father takes out a TCHS brochure and shows it to his daughter. The marketing piece offers photos of babies looking for mommies and daddies. "I was a commodity," Patricia says. "I was part of her inventory."

*One of Patricia's favorite family mementos, this framed
photo of her with her adoptive parents sits in the bedroom of
her retirement apartment. "I always felt like I was born
under a lucky star," Patricia says of her adoption and
escape from poverty.*

Larisa and Howard reassure her, though, over and over
again, that she is precious. Out of twenty-five babies, *she* was
the chosen one, they tell her. The little girl next door? Well,
that child's parents *had* to take her home from the hospital.

Later, in high school, a friend tells Patricia that her adoption
was the talk of the neighborhood: "My parents knew all about
the baby who was coming. It was such a big deal. They were so
excited."

Despite the love her adoptive parents lavish upon her, she
feels somehow different. It's a sense that is hard to pinpoint.
She's just different.

In the fourth grade, she turns for advice to her friend Lucille's grandmother, who lost a son in World War II. The

woman lives upstairs in Lucille's home, and her room becomes a type of after-school sanctuary for ten-year-old Patricia. "It just happened. She'd tell me about her son she lost in the war, and I would talk to her about being adopted. I remember sitting there, and I remember crying."

As an adult, Lucille says her grandmother intuitively knew that Patricia needed to talk. "My mother and I had no idea what you talked about."

"She was my first therapist," Patricia says. "She was the first person I talked to about being adopted, being different. She gave me permission to talk about things I didn't talk to anyone else about."

Despite wondering where she came from, Patricia, an only child, embraced her life. True, her birth mother turned her back on her at birth, but her adoptive mom always had her back. Always. "She was one of those amazing women who everyone adored. She was the answer gal. You only get one mother in this world . . . The one who sends you off to school, stays up late to wait for you." If you're fortunate.

Her adoptive father, Howard, is a sentimental man who spoils her. When her elementary school friends go away to summer camp, her father does not like—not one bit—the idea of her going, too. Although she and her mother talk him into it, he refuses to accompany her to the bus to say goodbye. At camp, she gets a postcard from him daily. Each one starts, "Dear Darling Daughter Patricia." Every time parents are allowed to call, an announcement on the loudspeaker summons her. Her father is on the phone. He always has the same message: "Just say the word, Dolly, and I'll bring you home."

She softens as she talks about him. "How lucky was I? He worshipped the ground I walked on. I could do no wrong. I knew that my life was beautiful."

Larisa dies of breast cancer when Patricia is only twenty-two, leaving an emptiness that makes her wonder how she will go on. "My mom affected everyone she came into contact with . . . She was bigger than life . . . She was an excellent model for caring for people, for being herself. She made everyone laugh."

In Howard's later years, after he has retired from the shoe industry, he helps Patricia open a candy and gift-basket business and runs it with her. "I was much loved . . . It's the good stuff that life is made of."

A beeping interrupts her memories, and she apologizes and adjusts a small cell phone–looking medical monitor on an end table. "Would you like more coffee?" We pause for a refill before returning to the story.

After Larisa's death, nearly thirty years pass before Patricia sees a TV exposé about the Tann adoption scandal. Her father, by then in his late eighties, catches her off guard when he mentions that he watched the program.

"Did you see it?" he asks.

She acknowledges that she did.

"I want you to know that Mommy and I never paid any money for you."

Her tone is wry as she describes that conversation to me. "Which was a massive lie," she points out. Like most parents, Larisa and Howard paid fees well above what a regular Tennessee adoption would have cost. They had money and would have given almost anything for their precious Dolly.

The TV program and a flurry of other reports about Tann in the early 1990s move many adoptees to seek their biological families. Patricia is not among them. She has no interest in connecting with her birth family—or so she tells herself. Instead, she focuses on resolving other relationship issues. Divorced young—with one child and while expecting another—she remains friends with her children's father, her only husband. She then becomes involved in a long-term relationship that ends badly and leads her to therapy. "One more thing we need to address . . ." her therapist says after many sessions.

Though as a child she willingly discussed her feelings about adoption with her friend's grandmother, Patricia is not willing to go there again during therapy. "I didn't talk about the adoption," she says. "There's that little spot in the corner of your heart . . . I wouldn't peek through that curtain very often."

The therapist persists: "You need to honor your history. You have to find your roots."

Instead, Patricia signs up for an intense weekend program with a different therapist, determined to get over the romantic relationship. A group of strangers sit in a circle to share and work through their innermost problems. As her fellow participants speak, Patricia is reminded of something Larisa used to tell her: "If everyone put their troubles in a hat, you'd want your own." That's the way she feels. "My story was nothing compared to what we heard."

Then one of the participants starts talking about his mother. Patricia begins to weep.

"Before I knew it, it was all about abandonment. All about my mother."

The group leader speaks words to her that no one has before: "When you're adopted, you come into the world with loss."

With an abundance of tears and tissues, Patricia goes well beyond an aha moment. The weekend is a breakthrough. "Being adopted does affect you," she realizes. She lingers on the thought now. "Mother loss . . . it's big-time stuff."

After Howard dies, Patricia hesitantly sends a letter to the

Tennessee Department of Human Services, requesting her birth records. "Take your time," she tells the officials there, not at all sure she wants to know her history. When she first hears back, the clues are few—and the Internet is not yet available for public research. She receives the name of her birth mother, a street in Nashville, and the bakery where her mother worked.

Having grown up in New York, Patricia, at this time of her life, still nurses a deep prejudice against the South—largely driven, she confesses, by fear of the unknown parts of her history. "I'm not proud of it, but that's how I felt." She picks at each of the scant details she receives about her birth mother, finding her first name, Anita, to be a singular, pleasing detail. It's one of the few kind thoughts Patricia remembers having that day. The mental stereotype she paints of her mother— seven hundred pounds, without a tooth in her head, and cooking up moonshine in the backyard—embarrasses her now.

She makes a decision as she reads the materials. She will not pursue her biological family further.

That pronouncement does not sit well with a group of soul-deep friends who have been part of her life since childhood. They are disappointed. They've daydreamed for years that Patricia is Jackie O's sister . . . or maybe Natalie Wood's. They also love Patricia enough to believe that she needs answers.

A friend who is headed to Nashville on business resurrects the subject. She phones Patricia and puts forth an oh-so-casual question: "What was that name again?"

Patricia answers, but she is swift to add, "I don't want to find her."

The friend writes down the information anyway and, posing as Patricia, calls every person with that name in the Nashville phone book. "My mother worked at Holsum Bakery," she says, and mentions Anita's name. Then she explains that she is trying to find others who worked there. After numerous tries, she makes contact with a guy whose mother was employed at the bakery.

Patricia is part amused and part irritated when she tells me what happened next: "I'm on my phone at home in New York when the operator breaks in with an emergency call."

It is her friend with information about the Nashville conversation.

That is an emergency? Patricia is peeved. "I don't want to hear it!"

The friend tells her that the man she reached on the phone gave her a number for a possible relative. Patricia hesitantly writes the number down—and puts it away, still afraid of what she might find. Having been given away at birth, she has always felt as if she missed being hit by a freight train by only an inch, that somehow she had escaped a bad life.

Months pass into a year.

Then this same friend begins working on her again: "Did you ever make that phone call?"

"You know damn well I didn't."

"I'm hanging up. You call her now."

So she does. Just like that.

When a woman answers, a most pronounced Southern accent comes across the line. *Exactly what Patricia expected.* But Patricia presses on, telling the stranger that she is looking for her birth mother. "I was born on Christmas Day 1942," she explains.

"Well, that just can't be," the woman drawls. "You got your story wrong, lady."

Patricia is more than eager to hang up. "I'm sorry I bothered you," she says. And she means it.

Then the woman gasps. "Lordy, Lordy, you're baby Carol."

The woman, twang and all, is Patricia's biological first cousin. Once upon a time, Aunt Anita arrived at her childhood home to recuperate after a mysterious baby was born. Cousins had huddled on a staircase to eavesdrop, sensing drama playing out.

Among things they overheard: Anita describing how hurt she felt at giving her child away, how hard it was to leave the baby.

Patricia is flummoxed. But the cousin's more meaningful news comes next:

"You have sisters."

"I do?"

For the first time, she feels a shiver of excitement about her birth family. For the first time, she learns the truth. The young Jewish mother who died and the med student father who couldn't keep the baby? They never existed. In truth, Anita was thirty-five when she became pregnant with baby Carol. She had four children at the time, and three who had died. She sent the four older children, who had no idea about a new baby, out West to stay with an aunt, who, decades later, held on to the secret.

The news of sisters causes a new round of doubts to swirl around Patricia. She ponders. She considers. She deliberates. Maybe she will call them. *Maybe not.* They can have a nice chat and exchange photographs and holiday cards. *Nothing more.* She is not getting involved with them.

But she cannot shake it. The time has come to make another call she is not sure she wants to make.

Her demeanor is luminous as she describes this moment. "I did find my sisters in 1992, these amazing, lovely sisters," she says of that phone call. "I found my family . . . I'm a very blessed woman."

The sister who answers the phone that day is in her late fifties—and confounded. "Where is this coming from? How could she have a baby and us not know about it?"

That sister hangs up and calls the oldest, who is in her sixties.

Patricia quickly receives a call from her.

The story told by the eldest is a heartbreaker. She and her three siblings were not given away. While Patricia grows up pampered in New York, they experience searing neglect. They are not parented. They grow up believing that if they try hard enough, dance fast enough, their mother will care.

One brother dies saving another brother from drowning. That brother is later killed in the Korean War. Tall for her age, the oldest sister lies to get a job as an elevator operator at age fourteen and buys cheap food, bologna mostly, for the children to eat each night. Meanwhile, Patricia has outfits for special occasions, including her all-time favorite chiffon dress. Her oldest sister has one dress, bought for her by an aunt. At sixteen, she marries and takes her nine-year-old sister to live with her and her husband. Even after that, life is difficult.

They never dream that one day they'll be reunited with a sister, a family secret revealed. The aunt who held that secret, who helped conceal the existence of baby Carol for so many years, eventually connects with Patricia as well. "I made a promise to your mother," she says of her reluctance to talk.

More chats between the sisters follow, but Patricia does not want an in-person meeting. Phone visits satisfy her, and she laughs with delight as she tells of an early conversation. Her oldest sister asks what church she belongs to.

"I belong to a synagogue, a temple, because I'm a Jew," Patricia responds.

Dead silence.

Then the sister says, "One of my neighbor's daughters down the street married a Jew. He is a lovely boy."

Patricia laughs more, remembering that awkward getting-to-know-you moment. Born to a Christian mother, she is now thoroughly Jewish, from her religious beliefs to holidays and family traditions. Her grandchildren call her Bubbe, using the Yiddish word for "grandmother."

All four are being raised in the Jewish religion.

Her sisters tell more stories of their upbringing and send photographs, including one of her birth mother, Anita. Patricia is shocked. "I saw my face looking at me, but she had the saddest eyes I had ever seen. That picture is so telling. I felt so sad for her." She shows me the image, her face filled with compassion. "How can you not feel for this woman?"

Patricia's sisters, after sharing photos and history, getting acquainted across so many miles, cannot take it anymore. They are impatient to meet her in person. "Can we come to Buffalo to visit?" they ask. She agrees to a visit but tells herself—and her friends—that this does *not* mean she is making a lasting connection with them.

Relating the story of seeing her eldest sister for the first time makes Patricia's eyes glisten once more. For so much of her life, Patricia felt as though she was not truly related to anyone. Now she has sisters. And they are visiting her. "I just remember touching her hand and feeling flesh of my flesh," she says. Her sister is the kindest, sweetest, and most beautiful person she has ever known.

And they share the same hands.

"They looked just like mine. I remember unfolding her hand and touching it . . ."

As for the sisters, they cannot believe how much she looks

like their mother. Plus, Patricia's upbringing intrigues them. "Are you going to make us a Jewish meal?" they ask.

"I'll cook you a brisket," she answers drolly.

Her sisters make biscuits and gravy for breakfast. Patricia cooks her famous brisket for dinner, and her youngest daughter is there for the visit. "It was just magical," Patricia says. "Of course, my friends all came."

She yields to enjoying these new family members, and that is the beginning of her deep relationships with her sisters, connections that enrich her life. They share laughs and spats and joys and heartaches, like all families. They are in touch all the time. Patricia's daughters, now grown, embrace their new aunts and cousins and their mother's unexpected family. Off at college when the first meeting occurs, her older daughter has a surprise awakening to what this means for her and her sister. She walks toward the new family photos, on display on a wooden side table. Then she hesitates and peers at her mother before she looks at the pictures. Patricia remembers her words well:

"Mom, I just want you to know this is your experience. We are so happy for you, and we think it's so interesting, but this is not our story. It's your story."

Then she picks up a photo of Patricia's brother who died in the Korean War. Her eyes widen. Huge tears roll down her cheeks. "He looks exactly like me," she says. "How could that be?"

In that moment, her daughter realizes that this isn't just Patricia's story after all. Nor are the stories of other TCHS adoptees only their stories. Their children and grandchildren and those yet to be born will carry part of that legacy in the color of their eyes, in the gestures they use, and in the traditions they follow.

A face-to-face meeting with Anita will never happen for Patricia, though. By the time the sisters reunite, she has died. Patricia is relieved. "I never met my birth mother," she says. "I did not want to meet her, and I think God knew that."

Nonetheless, Anita's story causes Patricia to cry as she sits in her apartment with me. Her birth mother wasn't a bad person. She is certain of that. Anita was simply unlucky. Patricia learns from her sisters that Anita was sexually abused while working in the cotton fields at age ten. Patricia has no idea who her biological father is.

In her later years, Anita exhibited signs of dementia and murmured almost in despair to her two other daughters, when they visited her in the care facility where she ended her days, "Where's that baby? What happened to that baby?"

They had no idea who she was talking about.

Patricia speaks softly to Anita's picture as she tells me this part of the story, as though she and her birth mother are alone in the room: "Thank you for having the courage to give me up. You may not have known that it was your finest moment, but it was."

The sibling circle that was broken on that day is sweet in its rebonding, decades later. The group—three sisters and their families—gather for a big reunion in a condo in the mountains of Colorado. Patricia writes a sister ceremony and gives each of them a bracelet, not unlike the ones she will later read about in *Before We Were Yours*. "I opened my heart up wide and let them in. They held on tight to me."

Both of her sisters, Patricia tells me, her voice husky, have since died. As she reflects on their missed years, she pulls out a small collection of photographs. They are among her most precious belongings, items she kept while giving her daughters many of her mementos. Her face shines with joy as she holds out a picture. "I'm so happy I can show you my sisters."

Their life together was not long enough, but Patricia feels fortunate for the time they had. Perhaps the harder burden is her regret for their rough upbringing. "My parents would have been so thrilled to have them, too . . . Anita was so lost. So sad. My parents would have had compassion for her." Even in her joy, there is grief over what could have been, the opportunities lost. Then she moves forward. "I had a charmed life. I had the best parents," she reminds both of us.

A few years ago, on a trip back to Buffalo, Patricia made sure they knew that, as well. Stopping by the cemetery where her adoptive parents lie buried, she placed a stone on their graves, in the Jewish tradition, to show she had been there. Her whispered message for them that day was the same as it is on this day, when she shares her story with me . . . and with the world.

"Thank you, Howard. Thank you, Larisa . . . thank you, thank you, thank you."

HIDDEN ROOMS
OF THE HEART

———

*P*atricia and I part with the embrace of friends who have shared heartache and emerged with hope. Her energy has waned, and I have a flight to catch. We would love to meet again in Memphis for the reunion in a few weeks, although we both know that's probably not possible—but we refuse to dwell on that.

As I hop into an Uber to the airport, my emotions are raw. Even for those adoptees who landed in the best situations after the Tennessee Children's Home Society, a haunting sense of being different hung in the air, a whiff of things that shouldn't be talked about. Of unanswered questions and unspoken secrets. Of searching hearts.

My thoughts linger on Patricia as a girl, the child who found a refuge for her secrets upstairs at a friend's house, in the room of an elderly woman who had lost a child in the war, a woman who also needed to talk. People come along when we need them and guide us on our journey. Enriching us.

Patricia has done that for me with her affection and good humor and sweet spirit. An unexpected stop at this point on my journey, she has helped me get my bearings and has renewed my faith in what will happen at the reunion ahead.

From here, I'll make a detour to connect with an adoptee in Florida, then head home to wash clothes, repack suitcases, pick up my patient husband, and drive cross-country back to Tennessee to do a few interviews in advance of the reunion.

But before we hit the road, I'll settle into the worn, overstuffed chair in my office, prop my feet on the ottoman, download some favorite music, and read through my notes from Patricia for encouragement and perhaps a bit of a road map for the interviews to come.

CHAPTER 8

A POLITICAL BABY

———

"I was a pretty little thing."

I T'S 1933. THE GREAT DEPRESSION GRIPS THE NATION. IT IS particularly hard on the rural South. To the already poor, it is devastating.

Beth Lee is a member of just such a family. Fifteen years old. Packed into a home with eight other children and little money, she is flattered by the attention of a man in his twenties. He's handsome. He's older. One thing leads to another.

She finds herself pregnant and unmarried.

On May 6, 1933, she gives birth to a baby girl, a child she is determined to keep. To give the child a surname, Beth's brother's best friend marries her. For nearly two years she and the baby stay in the family's crowded home. But Beth's father has little work, and her parents finally insist that the baby be given up for adoption.

Beth argues, but her parents overrule her.

She reluctantly hands her two-year-old daughter over to Georgia Tann and the Tennessee Children's Home Society in Memphis.

One mother's loss is about to become a wish fulfilled for a young couple in a small town in Tennessee. On the morning of

June 2, 1935, the couple receives the phone call they have been waiting for. The Children's Home Society has a toddler Tann thinks they will like. The little girl is available now.

The new mother, Geneva, would have preferred a boy. The father-to-be, Martin, a well-known member of the Tennessee State Legislature, wants a girl, and he is delighted. They jump into the car and make the 170-mile drive to Memphis that afternoon.

Martie

EAGER TO TALK WHEN I REACH HER ON THE PHONE, MARTIE Webster has only fifteen minutes. At age eighty-five when we visit, she lives in a retirement home, and an aide is coming to get her for dinner in the dining room.

But she has some important things she wants to say.

"I was born Margaret Jane," she says. "I've had a good life."

The aide stops by. "I'm on an important call," Martie tells her, then signs off with instructions for me to call her back. "I enjoy telling the story. I think it's right interesting. It's a pity that everyone is gone."

I call back at the appointed time, safely after the dinner hour.

Miss Martie is the oldest Tennessee Children's Home Society adoptee I am making plans to interview. She's not up to the trip to Memphis, and so we arrange for me to visit during what I've come to think of as my Rambling Road Trip. A few days later, she calls to say she will be having hip replacement surgery and cannot meet on the date planned. Just as disappointment settles in my stomach—she was someone I was so looking forward to meeting in person—she quickly suggests another time. Since she cannot meet on Monday, the day she will have surgery, might I come on Sunday?

On the scheduled date, I leave my Tennessee grandchildren and my husband swimming in the Nashville hotel pool and head south, struck by how the area has grown. After a grocery store stop for flowers (for Miss Martie) and a soft drink (for me), I drive to her building, a hospitable-looking place with an upstairs porch in a warmly Southern style. I ride up on the elevator with one of her neighbors and an aide who insists, in the friendliest way, on showing me to the correct door.

My hostess comes forward to greet me, pushing a small wheelchair, and expresses pleasure at the little pot of roses, then shows me around her compact space. She has lived here about a year, and it's all the room she needs. "I was having a hard time at home," she says, her old house too big for her to take care of anymore.

Her retirement home apartment sports intricate needle-work she's created, as well as family heirlooms. She even made the stunning—and remarkably difficult, to my eye—bird quilt on her bed. Her cross-stitched Mona Lisa smiles from a frame. The rocker and antique dresser were her adoptive mother's. "It was hard to decide what to bring up here," she admits. The only thing missing is her precious Yorkie, who lived in the apartment for two weeks, then went to stay with friends. "I just couldn't take care of her." Martie's voice is heavy with sadness. "I've been to see her once."

We sit in the living room, Martie settling into her wheel-chair across from the sofa, the day before her hip surgery. A family photograph watches over us from the wall behind her as she begins to tell her story. Even at her age, it is clear that what happened at the hands of Tann remains with her each day. "I think of myself as being a caring woman. I love animals . . . they call me Sunshine here. I love my family," she says, then hesitates. "I've always been self-conscious about my looks. I do think it's because deep in my mind I think, 'My mother gave me away.'"

With most of her life past, this delightful woman is frank but not careless with her words. So I am both surprised and sad when she remarks that she has never believed in herself. "I've never been a person who had the confidence I should have had. I felt beneath." Her voice is fervent when she speaks of Tann. "I know one thing . . . she was a cruel woman. I never have said this about anyone, but I hope she rots in hell for what she did."

Still, Martie believes that she was one of the fortunate ones. "I think I was very lucky to be adopted. If I had stayed in that family, I don't think I would have turned out okay." A few weeks before, her contradictory sentiments would have struck me as odd, but I've already learned that an ambivalence runs deep within many TCHS adoptees. For all the pain of the circumstances of their adoptions, they have processed enough about their backgrounds to know that if they had not been adopted, they would most likely have lived with other kinds of heartache.

Her earliest memories are of her adoptive father and days that were fun and carefree. "He took me everywhere he went when he was electioneering," Martie says. "He loved me so much and wanted to show me off . . . I'm not bragging, but I was a pretty little thing then. Georgia Tann preyed on the pretty little girls and boys." Even now, she has no idea how much money her parents paid to make her adoption happen. "I'll wonder to my grave if they bought me." In a tragic turn, her adoptive dad died at age thirty-four. "He was awfully young. Awfully." Martie was not quite six at the time. "When Daddy died, I was just fixing to start to school . . . I don't remember a whole lot about him, but I know he loved me a lot . . . I can still see him coming home with two ice cream cones, one for me and one for a friend."

Given up by her teen mother whose family couldn't afford to keep her, Martie is adopted by a well-to-do couple, but her adoptive father dies when she is almost six.

His death, in Nashville, was ruled a heart attack, yet she still wonders. "He took sick all of a sudden."

She describes her frantic parents returning to the Noel Hotel, where they're staying when the incident happens. Her mother, Geneva, sends her to the "picture show" while a physician attends to her father. "There's not much I remember about that day at all. I remember his funeral. I don't remember much about him. I wish I did. Mother said I went into a deep depression."

Although Martin's obituary mentions his "adopted daughter," she doesn't know that at the time. She is still too young to read. "I tell you how I found out I was adopted . . . there was a girl in my class in first or second grade. She called me *'dopted* and said it like it was a dirty word." Martie pauses. "We had a housekeeper named Eddie . . . a woman of color that I loved dearly. In fact, I thought *she* was my mother because she was with me more than my mother."

At the time, they live across the street from the elementary school, and when things don't suit Martie, she runs home. After being called *'dopted* on the playground, she hurries over to Eddie, upset. The beginning of the truth comes out. "'Miss Geneva won't tell you, so I'm going to . . .' she said. She sat me down and told me what 'adopted' was. She made it sound real pretty . . . I was something *picked*, not something you had to keep."

Years later, Martie runs into the girl who bullied her in elementary school. That girl, now an adult woman, does not remember the teasing and is chagrined. "Why would I have done that? I adopted a boy," she says.

The housekeeper's words may have comforted Martie in grade school, but they do not stick. She grows up feeling never quite accepted. She has the sense that her mother regrets the adoption after Martin is gone. "Me and my adopted mother did not get along sometimes," she says. "She was very bossy. I loved her, of course, and I think she loved me." But she seemed domineering. "I don't know if it was because I wasn't her child . . ." Miss Martie meets my gaze with sadness.

In addition, she recalls feeling that her adoptive grandparents do not accept her because she is not their blood relative. "You're not family," Martie remembers her granny telling her when she was in her early teens. Even all these years later, she carries the pain of those words. "I think that hurt as much as anything in my life."

The sense of rejection becomes a catalyst for wanting to find her birth mother. By this time, Martie is married and a mother herself. Tennessee's adoption records are still sealed, but her adoptive mother's second husband is a judge, and he helps her get the papers.

That's how Martie finally learns the name of her biological mother. She calls her by her first name, Beth, as she settles into this part of her story. "And my other mother, 'Mother,'" she adds, clarifying the difference matter-of-factly, as though everyone has two mothers. With her husband, she makes two trips to Memphis to try to find her birth family. "We just gave up. We didn't know how to do it."

While most TCHS adoptive parents want nothing to do with such a search, her adoptive mother, Geneva, travels to Memphis with Martie and other family members to try again. "They took the children to the zoo. Mother and I each got into a phone booth, each with a roll of dimes. I think every adoptee wants to know where they came from. Mother was all for it." They begin to call people with her birth mother's maiden name or married name. Finally, they track down the man whose name Martie carried before being adopted. They make contact, only the information he reveals is not what she expected.

"I was married to her, but I was not your daddy," he tells her. The best friend of her birth mother's brother, he'd wed Beth to give Martie a last name. Now, on this day, he once more provides assistance and leads them to her uncle. They connect, and Martie gets the information she has hungered for. "My uncle showed me a picture of my mother. I thought she was beautiful." Then she adds, with an endearing smile, "Unfortunately, I don't look like her."

By the time they find Beth, in about 1961, she has remarried, and she and her husband live in Las Vegas. Martie is nearly thirty and happy to receive a response from her. "Within a week, she came to see me," Martie recalls. Their reunion, scary and hectic, occurs at the Tennessee home of Martie's adoptive mom, Geneva. "Mother welcomed her with open arms," Martie says, "and let her stay the night."

Hearing Miss Martie describe the scene is poignant. She and her biological mother hug and kiss. "We looked each other over pretty good. I loved her instantly." A renewed relationship begins that day, and Beth even winds up living with Martie in the final months of her life. "She wasn't motherly. She was more sisterly. That's the way I felt toward her. She'd never been my mother."

They share stories. The past is rehashed.

In another cruel twist, Beth reveals that she looked for her lost daughter for years, then finally gave up. TCHS told her that her daughter had died. "After she was told that, she was so sorry she gave me up," Martie says. "I had a hundred questions I would have liked to ask her, but she was very reluctant. She never would talk about it as much as I wanted."

Beth is especially unforthcoming about Martie's biological father. All she will reveal is that she met the guy and fell for him. "She was fifteen . . . and him being a man . . . well, I think that's enough said." Miss Martie couches this fact in the language of a proper Southern lady.

She chose not to look for her father, but through her life she has seen men and wondered, " 'Could that be my daddy?' That's something else I used to think as I walked down the street. 'Is that my brother?' 'Is that my sister?' " She is sad when she learns that she has no siblings. Neither her adoptive mother nor her birth mother ever had other children.

Like so many TCHS adoptees, she is an only child.

Her adoptive mother dies in 2003, although Martie is fortunate to have had a phone conversation with her shortly beforehand. "I was always glad I had that last talk with her," she says. Martie's first husband, Hugh, and her birth mother both die in

2004. She remarries, and then this husband also passes away. Her tone becomes quietly reflective as she discusses this. "I've lost two husbands, two mothers, my car, my independence, my health . . . but I've gained a lot."

She has made friends at the retirement center and hears from her children regularly. They pop in and tell her about their lives, and motherly love radiates from her as she talks about them. The difference in the way she feels about her children and her emotions surrounding her upbringing are stark. "I wouldn't have given one of mine up. I'm very proud of my children . . . very, very proud." She smiles a little sheepishly. "Maybe too proud."

Martie has clearly thought a great deal about her adoption, repeatedly asking a question for nearly eight decades, a question echoed by so many other TCHS adoptees: "Even though I understand why she gave me away—I don't blame her—but I don't see how she could do it. I've never come to terms with it, even now. It hurts to know she gave me up. How could anyone give away their baby?"

THE WHY AND HOW

*O*n my way to the retirement home parking lot after visiting with Miss Martie, I pass two residents enjoying a conversation near the front door. A walker gets away from one and rolls downhill. I retrieve it, wondering about the stories of these two women's lives. I learned long ago that everyone has a story, and that we need to listen to more of them.

I sit in my car for a moment, reflecting on precious Miss Martie. Despite her birth mother's painful decision those long years ago, Miss Martie forged a loving family of her own. She moved forward with determination. I wish she were able to join us in Memphis for the reunion. Other adoptees would love meeting her and would understand what she has lived through. Together they could wrestle with the *how* of TCHS adoptions.

How does someone choose to prey on the most vulnerable? Go against all the instincts we have to protect children and market them like products? How does a community turn a blind eye?

How does a birth mother survive relinquishing a daughter she's raised for *two years*? And then survive being told that her daughter has died?

Those are questions no interview can fully answer.

Before I can put the car into reverse, my cell phone rings, and I see Miss Martie's number. When I answer, she tells me that she hopes we will stay in touch. "I enjoyed our afternoon very much," she says, "and I don't want to lose you."

I don't want to lose you either, Miss Martie.

And I know I won't.

We never lose those whose stories remain with us.

———

On the interstate drive back into Nashville, I crank up the air-conditioning. As I enter the city, I ponder how many people here in the state's capital have some connection to Georgia Tann's scandal. From adoptees to parents to lawmakers and bureaucrats, the numbers touched by TCHS seem enormous.

But my next interview is the day after tomorrow, outside either of these influential cities. I'll be back in the car for more Tennessee back-road travels, and I'm fairly certain that this adoptee will say that his life was also improved by his TCHS adoption.

At the moment, though, I'm anticipating Mexican food with two granddaughters and vow to hug them extra tightly.

CHAPTER 9

A HOLLYWOOD LIFE

"They looked at some kids and chose me."

W HEN THE TEENAGE GIRL ARRIVES AT THE BETHANY HOME
for Unwed Mothers in West Tennessee, she has not been told
exactly what awaits. That the moment her baby comes, she is
expected to sign it away.

On her sixteenth birthday, April 20, 1940, she labors to
bring a tiny boy into the world. He has her red hair.

Georgia Tann visits personally for an interview, but the girl
is intransigent. In no uncertain terms, Tann informs her that it
will be better if she voluntarily gives her baby up for adoption.
Like many young, unwed mothers who deal with the powerful
Tann, the girl struggles with the decision. Unlike most of the
others, she finds the courage to refuse to sign the paperwork.

She won't surrender her child.

It doesn't matter. The baby is taken anyway, as regularly
happened in this day and age, the decision not left to a vulnerable unwed teen, particularly when Tann was involved. The
newborn son becomes a ward of the Tennessee Children's
Home Society and is put up for adoption.

The young mother is allowed to remain at the unwed mothers' home for only a month. From there, she is sent to the Chattanooga Home for Wayward Women.

A place that will become, for her, a type of prison.

Stephen

STEPHEN SMILEY BURNETTE, AGE SEVENTY-EIGHT WHEN I meet him, is a cowboy reared in Hollywood, where Tann was a regular visitor in his childhood home. He grows up calling her "Memphis Tann." His adoptive father is the late Smiley Burnette, a famous cowboy actor, songwriter, and singer who made people laugh with his homespun humor and had many roles in Westerns and on television shows such as *Petticoat Junction*. Smiley was also the sidekick of Gene Autry, one of the most famous singing cowboys of all time and a pioneer in country music.

Stephen and his three siblings are among a substantial number of Southern babies sent to famous people in California, one of Tann's specialties. Smiley's traveling shows take him in and out of Memphis early in his career, and when his wife, Dallas, learns that she cannot have children, they choose two daughters and two sons from TCHS. They give each of the boys the middle name Smiley.

My trail to Stephen reminds me of tracking down leads in my days as a cub reporter. Journalism skills, some of them honed in a town not far from where I eventually find him, help me out. The Burnette adoptions are not a secret—a family photo appeared in a Memphis newspaper back in the day—but I learn about them from a TCHS adoptee who lives in Utah; he mentions that his parents were neighbors of the Burnettes in California and that Smiley connected his folks to Tann.

The names of many 1930s and 1940s movie and music stars

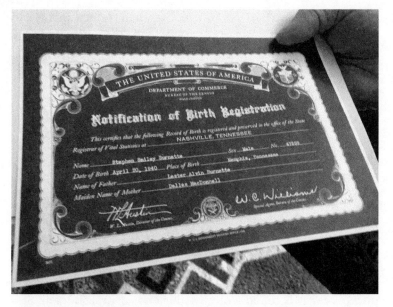

*Adopted by famous cowboy actor and singer Smiley Burnette,
Stephen calls Georgia Tann "Memphis Tann" during her numerous
visits to his childhood home. Smiley's real name is shown on
Stephen's birth certificate.*

may not mean much to me, but I do remember Smiley. My parents grew up in rural Arkansas in his era, and they loved his down-to-earth humor. He appeared as the train engineer in *Petticoat Junction*, one of my favorite shows when I was a girl. I even had a coloring book of the Hooterville gang—the type of item now sold online as a collectible. I tell myself that finding Stephen will be easy enough because he, his daughter, and a friend have lovingly maintained a Smiley website. They have not, though, kept up with their email response form—they got too many silly questions, Stephen tells me later.

But a mention I find on the Internet suggests that he lives in a small town in Tennessee—only twenty-five miles from my in-laws and a pair of our grandchildren. That would mean Stephen has returned to the land of his birth. I turn to the old faithful White Pages, which I scarcely use anymore, and find a Burnette. No one, however, picks up the phone to unrecognized callers these days. I suppose I can leave a message.

I punch in the numbers.

When Stephen answers, it takes me a moment to collect myself. "Are you . . ." My words sound awkward as I assure him that I am not a telemarketer.

"Yes . . ."

Well, then.

He is gracious as our conversation continues, in spite of suffering from a bad cold. He volunteers information I do not know about Tann. He even calls me back a couple of times to ask if I've been in touch with this person or that. He asks me to give his regards to old Hollywood friends if I reach them. Stephen is an intriguing mix of gruff and polite. "You're going to find out a few things," he says. "This is a long story."

I broach the subject of doing an in-person interview with him. He will have just had shoulder surgery the week before the TCHS reunion and does not seem to give the gathering any thought. But he is open to a visit while I am in the area. He is gregarious, even amenable to more phone chats. If he's around, he says, he'll answer and talk. As for scheduling an in-person interview? "You can do it anytime you want. I'm show business."

He offers up directions to his home with the insistence of a parent who wants to make sure I get there—and who does not trust GPS. *Exit here, not there. Left at the second stop.* I can't keep from smiling at his insistence and rely on my notepad, rather than my maps app.

He also puts me in touch with his actress daughter, Elizabeth Burnette, who has a long-running role on *Grey's Anatomy.* A smart, compassionate woman who is protective of her father, she vets me online after my initial call to him, including checking my website and Facebook page. After I talk with Stephen on the phone, she generously telephones me and speaks with love about her family, particularly her father. "I think he's an awesome person," she says with warmth.

I'M SO NERVOUS THAT I'll get lost out in the country that I am sweating by the time I arrive at the house where Stephen lives. In my defense, it is hot and humid in Tennessee in June, and there is road work at the turn to his place, which delays me for ten minutes. I have the idea that you do not want to keep Mr. Burnette waiting.

He welcomes me to the house he has shared for years with his cat, Smoky, and a couple who have been longtime friends and are the ultimate Smiley fans and collectors. Lush blue hydrangeas are in splendid bloom beyond the den window. There's a cornfield next door. His father and the *Green Acres* crew, from another of Smiley's shows, would feel at home out here.

Stepping into the house is like walking into a Smiley Burnette museum, memorabilia at every turn. From a replica of Smiley's star on the Hollywood Walk of Fame to framed movie stills, the presence of Stephen's adoptive father dominates. The items are soon woven into the conversation and offer a glimpse into another world, another way of life.

Stephen settles into his tale with the panache of a true Hollywood storyteller, but he carries himself more like a Tennessee farmer. He is dressed in blue work pants and a chambray Western shirt with snaps. On his feet he wears leather moccasins. He usually dons a cowboy hat, though indoors today his head is bare. He's recovering from his surgery, and it would be an understatement to say that he is not the most tolerant pa-

Stephen Smiley Burnette shows off the collection of his father's memorabilia at his home in West Tennessee. Smiley and his wife, Dallas, adopt two boys and two girls from Georgia Tann. Both sons are given the middle name Smiley.

tient. He fidgets with the sling and grouses about it to his friend who sits nearby. She fusses gently.

"Smiley came by Memphis on a tour. He loved Memphis," Stephen says. "He felt it should be the country music center of the state of Tennessee." From there the conversation moves to Dallas and Smiley's visit to TCHS, and Stephen's voice sounds matter-of-fact when he says, "They looked at some kids and chose me."

An actor and stuntman who seems still to long for that work, he has a big personality and, like all Tann adoptees I meet, a packet of paperwork to present. The memories he shares with me give a glimpse at the kind of life many people fantasize about.

If not for his Tann adoption, that life would never have been his.

SMILEY AND DALLAS ADOPT the baby boy when he is three and a half months old.

His adoption is never hidden. "I have always known," Stephen says. "So have the other three . . . Everyone knew it. Dad didn't want to be blackmailed, so he told everyone right up front."

His adoptive father becomes friends with Tann, who goes on to visit their home in Studio City, California. "She liked my dad because he was in Memphis a lot," Stephen says. That connection leads to Stephen often encountering her during his boyhood in California. "I've known Memphis Tann since forever. She used to come out and visit. She was delivering babies to other homes. It wasn't just a one-time thing."

Dallas and Smiley, good-hearted, trusting people, believed deeply in Tann's efforts to connect children with families; they did not know about her questionable adoption schemes until the scandal broke. Sometimes she would spend the night with them and fly back out of Burbank. One time when she came, she had delivered a couple of kids to neighbors on the same street, Stephen recalls. "Some people up the block got a good one," he says. "They adopted a second one who didn't work out and sent him back."

This is one of the complaints long held against Tann—that

she did not properly check homes and, as a result, the children were often set up to fail. Parents were permitted to return a child, like a piece of clothing that did not fit. Stephen, though, thinks more highly of her than most, as did his adoptive parents. "She didn't sell babies, per se," he says. "She would take three or four children to California, billing each family for the flight, hotel, and money for the comfort, health, and safety of the child."

Some see that as selling children, charging multiple times for the same flight and other expenses. Stephen doesn't share that opinion. "Nobody paid to get a baby . . . I can tell you how it was done. If you sent one welfare worker to California and charged a welfare worker times five, they said that was paying for the baby. It wasn't. It was just smart."

Whatever question I ask Stephen about the charges against Tann, he deflects with the certainty that overall she did a good thing for children. He feels strongly that she helped in a time when people—particularly unwed mothers—could not afford to keep their kids. "She did a whole lot for people in World War II," he says. "Think about it—there would have been a lot of kids turned out." And he does not believe she was taking money, although records and reports say she lived extravagantly on what she made through the orphanage, maintaining a luxurious home in the city, a limousine and chauffeur, a plantation farm outside Memphis, and a beach cottage for recreation. "Georgia Tann meant no harm," he tells me as we talk. "She was putting all her money back in the home."

He does, though, mention that "she was in very well with the mayor of Memphis." Her connections with that mayor, Boss Crump, allowed Tann to run her orphanage the way she wanted. But the good and evil of Georgia Tann adoptions are inextricably intertwined, as Stephen's perspective shows. It's a strange dichotomy that in many cases she crushed lives, while in other cases, she changed lives for the better. Stephen, who grew up in a happy home, clearly fits in the latter category.

The contrast between the life he might have had and the one he wound up with is a truth that has defined his life. Anybody who grew up with a Cadillac and a chauffeur was better off than a poor child in Tennessee, he points out. The Burnette home, on three-quarters of an acre, had a pool, workshop, blacksmith shop, and paint shop. "I grew up with advantages that a child in those days would have died for . . . I had all those things available to me."

Although his adoptive father might be more well known, young Stephen adores his adoptive mother, too. Eleven years older than Smiley, Dallas is warm, loving, and caring. She is not in show business but travels with Smiley in the early years.

Between ages seven and fourteen, Stephen is practically raised by an African American housekeeper, a circumstance echoed by others adopted into families with money. "She was kind of the person who grew me up . . . She was my go-to person. If I needed something or permission to do something, I would go to her when my parents were gone." He becomes emotional as he recalls another maid and driver being hauled off to a Japanese internment camp. "I remember them jerking them away from me."

His father does shows on the road to augment his film and TV income, and Stephen starts young in the family business. "I have one recollection at about four years old, going on the stage with Dad. Mom was offstage. Dad was proud of the fact that he had children," he tells me as he sits reminiscing in the comfortable den with the morning light filtering in. His cat wanders over to check me out, then to rub up against Stephen.

I've found Smiley's performances online. They are filled

with singing and jokes. They're old-fashioned and funny. He pauses during one set to mention his children, calling each by name, clearly proud, as Stephen has told me. "Smiley Burnette is happily married," he says in a long-ago performance in Fort Worth. Smiley goes on to talk about each of his children with affection. Listening to Smiley's material helps me see where Stephen acquired the open and engaging personality that carried him through an interesting life.

But even in the closest families, parents and children can have their differences. At age sixteen, wanting to be independent, Stephen runs away from home and ends up joining the Navy for four years. A paradox arises: he has left his adoptive parents behind, but his father's name continues to open doors, and Stephen is forthright about how references to his famous father benefited him through the years. Being Smiley's son helps get him into the Navy and college and saves him a traffic ticket or two when officers see his driver's license.

"It's kind of funny how who you are makes a difference," he remarks. He tells a story about dodging a run-in with the law while sharpening his knife as he was having his boots shined near Waco, Texas. A passing policeman thought that was peculiar behavior, possibly even threatening, and told Stephen, "Come with me, young man."

Ordered to identify himself, he pulled out his license, and the policeman inspected it. His middle and last names raised a familiar question: "Are you related to Smiley Burnette?"

"He's my dad."

"Why didn't you tell us that?" the officer asked, and left him alone.

He carried his dad's picture in his wallet after that.

Stephen is living in Texas, making fifty-two bucks a week at a gas station when Smiley comes through during a tour. His dad asks if Stephen wants to earn twice that by going on the road with him.

At twenty-one, he is reunited with his adoptive family and traveling with his father. He marries once in the early 1960s, has two children, and delays a divorce, in deference to Smiley. "He didn't want me to get divorced, so I didn't." Eventually, though, the couple splits up. Stephen never remarries.

To please his father and to earn a better paycheck, he sets up the show and helps in whatever way is needed. They do one-nighters, often traveling four hundred miles in a day to make the next performance. While describing this part of his life, he tosses out an unexpected piece of information: "During that time, I found out who my real mother was." Between shows in Minneapolis and somewhere in Louisiana, Stephen stops in Memphis, goes to the Vital Statistics office, and tells a clerk he wants his birth certificate. "She's got it in her hand," he says with a spark in his eyes.

But she will not turn it over.

"You're illegitimate. I can't give it to you," she says.

With his charm and connections always at the ready, he finagles a copy.

It is 1962 when he decides to look up his biological mother, with a need that has haunted him for years. "I knew I had a mother out there . . . adopted kids have an intuition they don't understand," he says, a sentiment I'd heard from other adoptees. When he sets out on his search, he has been on the road with Smiley, and it is between midnight and one A.M. Police pull him over in a small Arkansas town and want to know what he is doing. He produces his license, and his name works its magic. They ask him about Smiley, then proceed to escort him halfway to his birth mother's house. He had contacted his biological grandmother before coming, and his mother, Ruth, a hairdresser, is still up.

The late-night reunion clearly rocked him. "She was waiting for me because her mother had called her. She only asked me one question. I'd gone through years of trying to find her, and she asked me when I was born."

"April 20, 1940" is his answer. Her expression turns to joy. He and his mother share a birthday. April 20. His answer and their connection finally solve his lifelong mystery.

She cries. He doesn't. "I was too tough. I was twenty-one," he says dryly.

He also meets his grandparents and great-grandparents. His birth father is dead: a man, he is told, who was a relative by marriage. One more detail he finds out: he was conceived in a cornfield not unlike the one next door to his home now. After giving birth to Stephen and being trapped in the Chattanooga Home for Wayward Women for two years, Ruth turns eighteen and is unceremoniously shown the door. She is on her own. She winds up moving to California, completely unaware that the son taken from her when she was sixteen is growing up nearby. Along the way, she has another child and puts him up for adoption, too.

After she and Stephen reunite in Arkansas, the relationship matters more to him than perhaps he had expected. He wants more time with her and decides to stay in the small town. "All at once, I decided I wanted to live near her," Stephen says, and a hint of the searching young man he was shimmers just below the surface. Smiley, ever the good father, gives his blessing. "He was one to always let me do what I wanted to do." Stephen leaves Smiley's road show and remains with Ruth and her fourth husband for six months.

When Stephen cannot make a living in the small town, however, he joins back up with Smiley at the Seattle World's Fair. Ruth gives him her car to haul his trailer. After that, they call and write, and he visits her once a year. "They wanted me to put them in show business," Stephen remarks. The words sound wry.

Dallas also writes to Ruth after Stephen's reunion. "I had two mothers corresponding with each other," he says in a "that's odd" tone. He calls each of them Mom, and both matter to him and to his family, in different ways. They are part of his story, an example of the many lives unpredictably intertwined by a Tann adoption.

Stephen's daughter, Elizabeth, is close to his adoptive mother and grows close to his birth mother as well. She speaks compassionately of Ruth, her biological grandmother. "I had a great relationship with her . . . I knew her quite well. I got to ask her all the questions I wanted. She didn't want to give him up. That was her first baby."

Ruth told her, "I just prayed I would see him one day."

Elizabeth tells me that her father is the spitting image of his biological mom, right down to the red hair he hated as a child because he thought it was the same color as the carrot cake at his birthday party.

"You couldn't miss the resemblance between her and Stephen," Elizabeth says. Many things, like the red hair, now make sense. Old questions finally have answers. Yet when Elizabeth investigates other family ties, she's warned off by her father. "My dad told me to get out of that can of worms." And, as it turns out, not all the biological family members want to form attachments.

It's a very personal decision, and the reason, Stephen says, he ultimately chose not to pursue connecting his adopted siblings with their birth families. "When I found out who I was, I also found information about the birth parents of my two adopted sisters and brother. When I came back—I was on the road with Dad—I asked them, and they didn't want to know." He burned the information, convinced it was not his place to interfere.

Stephen develops a career in Hollywood: acting, working in production, painting, and being a stuntman. "It makes a living," he tells me. When Smiley is on *Petticoat Junction*, Stephen is working on a Western that future president Ronald Reagan directs. Reagan remarks to Stephen, "Did your dad ever tell you I was best man at his wedding?" Reagan then describes traveling along when Smiley and Dallas eloped to Santa Ana in the late 1930s.

"I didn't know it till Ronald told me."

I could listen to the stories of this man's unusual life for hours. But our time together is almost over. As I prepare to leave, we walk through the living room, foyer, and dining room, looking at items that tell of both Stephen's and Smiley's vibrant careers. One of Stephen's talents is the fast draw, and he points to the other side of the room, saying, "That's one of my holsters over there." For a particularly memorable job, the opening of *Gunsmoke*, he critiqued how the draw was done. He re-creates the scene verbally: "He draws and fires. That's horrible!" Stephen's advice, learned from a famous holster maker: "You don't throw your elbow out."

My *Petticoat Junction* coloring book springs to mind when I see a framed picture of Smiley in the show's signature locomotive.

Stephen's cowboy life makes him happy, and he is proud of being Dallas and Smiley's son, declaring, "I am a cowboy." He lets loose with a rakish grin, a glimpse of the young, redheaded stuntman who was quick on the draw, and tells me, "I'm a 'reel'—r-e-e-l—cowboy."

AN UNWRITTEN
SCRIPT

A bit of movie-star magic clouds my vision as I wind through the hills of Tennessee. After losing myself in the Smiley Burnette memorabilia and tales of Old Hollywood, it's easy to forget that the upcoming reunion will play out according to an unwritten script. Our gathering is now merely three days away, with six adoptees confirmed. So much else about it remains a question mark.

A nondescript tin utility building with a simple sign out front catches my eye, and I'm happy for the distraction. A good barbecue shack can cure a multitude of ills. I swerve into the drive-through, order a pulled-pork sandwich topped with signature Tennessee coleslaw, and find a spot to eat in the shade of a tree. I ponder how this state with so many things to boast of could have let these children down so completely.

From the Grand Ole Opry to the Smoky Mountains, Southern charm, and a lot more, Tennessee is known for so much good. And yet it kept the ugliness of Georgia Tann and the Tennessee Children's Home Society as much a secret as possible, never fully addressing the wrongs done to so many. Even as I conduct these interviews, those who want their records from TCHS adoptions are asked to pay fees that are too steep for aging people on fixed incomes.

For years, Tann survivors have made their own pilgrimages to this region in search of their roots. Perhaps in some way, their lives can never be fully separated from Memphis, from what happened here. I wonder if we are doing the right thing in inviting them back. Are we merely pointing them, once again, toward a pain they dealt with long ago?

This isn't Hollywood, after all. We don't get to write the script.

Who gets the last line? What does it say?

By this time next week, we'll know.

CHAPTER 10

LEFT TO DIE

———

*"I need to tell you that we got you
from a woman named Georgia Tann."*

Viola and Harold Parker make their way to the orphanage on Poplar Avenue, not far from their Memphis home. The weather is chilly enough for a jacket, but the sun shines brightly on this February day in 1947.

More than twenty years ago, the couple had suffered the loss of a daughter at birth, leading to a virulent infection and a hysterectomy for Viola. They still long for a child.

Today they have an appointment to get one.

With World War II behind them, they are now financially secure, the owners of a modest but thriving engineering firm and a small house in east Memphis. They realize, however, that they have waited too long to be eligible to adopt a child conventionally. In their mid-forties, the Parkers, like many older couples, have decided to turn to Georgia Tann and the Tennessee Children's Home Society to build their family. Harold, a civil engineer, works with civic employees at Memphis City Hall, a place where the well-known adoption matron has superb connections.

When they open the door to the orphanage, Tann herself greets them and exclaims that she has a wonderful baby for them. She leads them to a side room and shows them a healthy baby boy in a crib right near the door; there are several other cribs in the room.

Viola and Harold are overwhelmed by how rapidly events are moving. Tann has chosen this son for them. She picks up the child and shows him off with pride, giving one of her typical sales pitches to the eager customers.

But while she goes on about the virtues of the boy, a mewling sound drifts from a crib on the far side of the room. It's strange, almost like the cry of an animal.

Harold is distracted. "What's that noise?"

Tann, a strong-willed woman, does not hide her annoyance. Few people interrupt her, and even fewer thwart her. She attempts to direct Harold's attention back to the bouncing baby. "That's nothing. Look at this fine boy!"

The father-to-be, kinder than Tann is arrogant, elbows past her and the child in her arms. He is gripped by the faint distress call coming from the other side of the room. His wife follows. But they are steered away by Tann and an assistant.

Again the unsettling sound comes from the corner.

Shaking off Tann and her helper, Harold changes direction, insistently. Moving closer, he sees an infant quite different from the robust boy Tann has offered up. The pitiful, tiny thing lies untended in a corner crib. Her face and hairless head are covered with a crusted rash, and as she cries, Harold sees that the tip of her tongue is attached to her front gums. She appears too weak to move.

Harold, of a good heart, picks up the distressed baby. Tann tries once more to steer him back to the boy she's picked out. "Every man wants a son," she insists.

Harold will not be deterred. He looks more closely at the days-old infant, clearly neglected, her frail, strange-sounding cries deemed unworthy of attention. Overcome with pity, Harold and Viola declare that they'll take the girl: "We want this one to go home with us."

They pay five hundred dollars for her, more than seventy times the regular rate for a Tennessee adoption.

Lillian

"THE NOISE WAS ME," SAYS LILLIAN ROBERTS, A LIFELONG Memphis resident. "I was in the crib. I was thirteen days old. My tongue was tied. I was covered with a crusty rash and crying weakly."

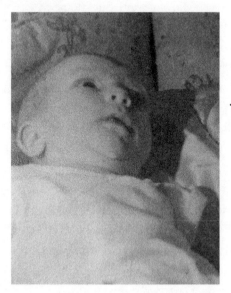

Tiny, sick baby Lillian is saved from the clutches of Georgia Tann by compassionate adoptive parents who choose her over a healthy child.

She is gracious when she returns my call requesting an interview. "I am a Georgia Tann baby," she says in her gentle

Southern accent on my voicemail. "I'm seventy-one years old, and I'd be most delighted to speak with you."

I call her back, and we set up a time to meet. Since she's in Memphis and I'll be heading there for the reunion, I schedule our interview for a day before others start arriving. She is quick to invite me to her home.

The sun is hot overhead, but Lillian's street is shady when I pull my rental car into her driveway. My pre-reunion nerves have reached maximum potency with my arrival in Memphis. I'm suffering from a mix of anxiety at asking yet another stranger deeply personal questions and wondering if the weekend activities will come off in the spirit intended.

But seeing the ranch-style house, the front door open, and Lillian awaiting me, I relax. She could be the lady in the next pew at church or the mother of a friend. She makes me instantly at home, a warm hostess who answers questions with grace and soft-spoken candor.

Although she has not moved far from TCHS through the years, the abandoned baby matured into a smart, caring woman who uses her experiences to help others. She has centered her life on faith and family; two children, one adopted and one biological; and grandchildren who live close enough to use her babysitting services. The welcoming home she and her late husband built together has aged nicely, in a well-established neighborhood with oak trees that own the yards. She leads me through a hall and into a cozy den decorated with family photographs. A container of fragrant white gardenia blossoms highlights the coffee table. A gardenia bush was growing in a neighbor's yard when Lillian was adopted. When she and her husband built their own home, they took a cutting and rooted it.

Like Lillian, it blooms still.

She is a retired advanced-math teacher who influenced many

a student during her teaching years. A mastery of math is, after all, a valuable thing. Even in her retirement, she devotes her life to serving. She regularly uses her cooking skills to prepare food for others, such as two hundred fifty pigs in a blanket for an upcoming bridal shower and homemade orange cake for Vacation Bible School. She's saved some of that cake for me and presents it with a pretty napkin and a china plate. She leads the homebound ministry for her church and escorts older friends on trips. She continues to help students with the ACT.

"I stay super busy," she says as we get to know each other.

Her daughter, Jill, has told me in a phone visit that she appreciates the way her mother gives and does things for others. "She's a Christian. That goes along with the Christian faith, to be a giver. She was raised to give." Jill has seen the gradual process of her mother adjusting to her troubling birth story. "I think she was definitely supposed to be with the family she was with. They shaped her into the person she is . . . me, too."

Lillian's adoptive parents were quietly religious, involved in a local church. "They took me to church every time the doors opened," she says. Through the years, that religious upbringing anchors her, although she is wary of preaching, choosing to show her faith through actions. "When you love God, he'll watch over you," she says. "Regardless of being rejected by people, I've been accepted by God . . . That helps make up for a lot of things in my life."

Taking a breath, her expression calm, she leans back against the sofa and opens the adventure of her life with "This is the story my dad told me . . ."

SHE WAS GIVEN THE NAME Rosie when she was born, on February 9, 1947, but her name is changed to Lillian after Harold and Viola wrest her from Tann's clutches. The name is chosen in honor of Viola's mother.

From the moment they hold her in their arms, her new parents love and care for their sick baby. An organized man, her father had already arranged a visit with a pediatrician friend. They'd expected to take their new baby boy in for a routine checkup on the way home from the orphanage. Just a precaution.

Instead, they arrive at the doctor's office with a sickly baby girl who's in dire need of an intervention. "Undesirable babies were sometimes left to die and be buried on the premises of Tann's TCHS. These babies had physical illnesses or deformities or were judged 'unworthy' or 'unattractive,'" Lillian writes in a two-page account of her life that she compiled for recent talks about *Before We Were Yours*. "I had been left in a corner crib, presumably to die because of my physical problems and unattractive appearance. My daddy's choice and my mother's sympathy most likely saved me from a backyard grave."

The doctor examines Lillian, and his diagnosis is swift. She is hungry, and her stomach hurts because she is allergic to cow's milk. The allergy is also the cause of the rash. Her strange cries are the result of having been born tongue-tied. The physician clips her tongue, prescribes ointment for the rash, and suggests a diet of goat's milk.

From that day forth, Harold begins adding regular trips to the country to his schedule, to buy goat's milk for this tiny daughter of theirs. Within days, she bears almost no resemblance to the pitiable creature left to suffer in Tann's orphanage. She is thriving.

Lillian grows up an only child in a quiet household, a tidy two-bedroom, one-bath home not far from the orphanage. An introspective little girl, she loves books and is given voice and speech lessons to help with her slight speech impediment. Her new parents are honest about her birth and read her a bedtime story about adoption most nights. *The queen and king had a baby and couldn't take care of it, so they gave it to a farmer and his wife.* As in the made-up tale, her adoptive parents grew up as farmers. They were from Mississippi and came from little in terms of money or possessions. Her new mother was a sickly child and quit school after the eighth grade. Her dad lived in poverty but came from a family of mechanical geniuses. He wound up enrolling at Ole Miss, acquiring the education that led to his career as an engineer.

Lillian as a schoolgirl. Raised as an only child, she knows she is adopted but does not learn the truth about her birth family for decades.

Harold is a calm man. Viola, a strict woman. Despite their love, as Lillian speaks of her childhood she recalls the feeling of not quite belonging. Once again, I hear those familiar words: *Something was missing.* In crowds during her growing-up years, she habitually looked to see if she could spot a sibling, anyone related to her. "I guess I always wanted a brother or sister," she says in her easy-on-the-ears Tennessee accent.

Even now, questions linger. But she is unruffled as she talks about her story and about how she came to be connected with *Before We Were Yours* and, eventually, the TCHS reunion. An avid reader, she is enmeshed in her busy life when she notices *Before We Were Yours* on the *New York Times* bestseller list and requests it from her branch of the Memphis library.

Not long after, a friend who knows about her family background invites her to speak about her life to a book club at Kirby Pines, a Memphis retirement community, with the author of *Before We Were Yours* participating on the phone from her home in Texas. Nearly a hundred book enthusiasts listen to Lillian's first public telling of her story, enraptured by the account of her life. "It's amazing how that worked out," she says. "I'm not going to preach a sermon, but I don't believe it was an accident." Since that day, she has given as many as three book talks a week, comparing and contrasting her life with that of the Foss siblings in the novel.

She keeps her adoption records in a tote bag, ready to go.

The novel and the talks bring emotions to the surface. "I think adopted children always have a piece of themselves missing. You're rejected at birth for something you had nothing to do with. I would love to know exactly what was in my birth mother's mind when she gave me up. Of course, I'll never know. I would like to think she wanted me to have a better life. I'd love to ask her, 'Why did you do this?'"

That question will become a specter in an otherwise comfortable life, something that quietly hovers over Lillian once she's old enough to understand what adoption means. As a child, she lacks self-confidence and is not outgoing. She remains a loner throughout her school years, migrating to one best friend at a time. A case of the measles strikes her in fourth grade, and she has to miss school. While some parents might have brought her Play-Doh or a Mr. Potato Head to play with, Harold entertains her by teaching her basic algebra. He gives her problems to solve while he is at work and goes over them with her when he comes home.

Her lifelong interest in math begins. Viola, however, is not a numbers person and cannot understand her daughter's fascination. Mother and daughter do not have much in common and butt heads as Lillian grows. Their disconnect doesn't have to do with love, Lillian insists, but stems from different interests. She learns young that, despite the childhood book about adoption, Viola does not want to talk about it. Even in adulthood, Lillian respects her mother too much to ask.

Instead, Lillian makes up her mind that only when her mother dies will she try to find out about her birth family.

Decades pass before she hears how she came to be in the orphanage the day she was rescued. Viola has died, and Harold has had a heart attack. After that, he opens up to her. "I need to tell you something," he says. "I need to tell you that we got you from a woman named Georgia Tann." He shares more details about the day she was left suffering in a corner crib, then was spared almost certain death by the tenacity of this now-frail man who raised her. By the kindness of strangers who would become her parents. Harold then tells her the name of her birth mother and the street where she lived when Lillian was born.

Just like that, missing pieces begin moving into place.

Lillian learns by accident how much her parents paid for her adoption. "Dad didn't mean to tell me. He was joking with me and said, 'That's the worst five-hundred-dollar investment I ever made. I should've taken Butch.'"

Why did they have to pay five hundred dollars when a Tennessee adoption was seven dollars at the time, and they picked the baby up themselves? And what happened to that cute little boy Harold turned down, the one he teasingly later referred to as Butch? Did the baby boy, too, stay in Memphis or was he sent to California or New York? Is he still alive?

There's no way of knowing.

In the early 1990s, when Tennessee's adoption records are finally opened and many adoptees and their families find themselves watching televised programs about Tann's misdeeds, Lillian is among those viewers who question their heritage. Straitlaced, she cannot fathom her birth mother having a child out of wedlock. She imagines instead that she was a stolen baby. Maybe her mother has been looking for her all these years.

On the East Coast, another woman sees the program, too, and because she does, Lillian's life is about to take a twist. The woman is Lillian's half sister Fran, a sibling Lillian has no idea exists. Fran is also a Tann baby, born one year to the day before Lillian. Confusion over their birthdays in state records leads her to Lillian. Fran's adoptive parents live in Memphis when she is born, but they want to get away from Tann, fearing being blackmailed into paying more money to keep their child. They move out of town as soon as the adoption is final, a not uncommon reaction for threatened parents who feel pressured by Tann.

Almost fifty years later, Fran's husband, having tracked details through the opened birth records, calls Harold. "Do you have a daughter who is adopted?" he asks.

"Yes." Lillian's father does not seem particularly startled by the question.

"Does *she* know she's adopted? I think she might be my wife's half sister."

Harold, aging and not in good health, is delighted by the news. His daughter will have someone else to love. "He was happy for me," Lillian says.

Fran collects all sorts of papers on her adoption and hands the materials over to Lillian, which helps her accept the truth of her own birth. "I had documentation," Lillian says. Then she adds, with a big smile, "Math teachers have to prove things." Still, she finds it almost impossible to believe that her mother, whose name was Barbara, had two babies with different fathers a year apart. Lillian speculates that she was an unhappy person who never got along with her own father and came to Memphis looking for love.

Over the course of regular, long phone calls, sister Fran becomes part of Lillian's life. Sadly, though, they are still kept apart. This time the barrier is not secrecy but distance and retirement finances. "I know her, and I love her—even though I've only seen her three times," Lillian says.

Years after she connects with Fran, Lillian decides to see what she can find out about her biological father. Another surprise awaits: the discovery of a second half sister, Joyce, with a shared father. Through an attorney, Lillian contacts Joyce, her dry sense of humor emerging as she describes the letter she sent: "I do not want anything from you," she writes. She wants her sister to know she is not an ax murderer and not after her kidneys. She does, however, seek medical information about her birth father.

She signs the letter with her birth name, including the last name she once shared with Joyce.

Then she waits.

The letter lands with a thud. Joyce responds to the attorney, saying her father, now dead, would never have considered having a child out of wedlock. "Why is that lady lying?" she writes.

After a while, though, Joyce seeks confirmation of the claims and asks that Lillian pay for a DNA test. Years ahead of mail-order-kit technology, the test costs three hundred dollars, money not easy to come up with. "That was a financial struggle for me," Lillian confesses. But she saves up and takes the test.

She waits again.

The results show Lillian and Joyce to be half sisters.

More waiting ensues.

Finally, Joyce agrees to a lunch date with Lillian, who is nervous. Lillian's daughter, a young adult at the time, encourages her. "Mom, where is your faith?" she says. "I'll go with you."

The meeting is stressful. "We talked," Lillian says. "It was very awkward . . . I did not want to cause her any distress at all."

While this sister keeps Lillian at arm's length, she does share copies of pictures, including a photo of Lillian's birth father. He was a sailor, then a civilian employee for the U.S. Navy. He, like her adopted father, worked with numbers. Lillian chuckles. "I ended up being a math teacher, so I think I got a double dose."

She now has two pictures of her birth parents together. One was taken at the Pink Palace, a museum in Memphis, in July 1946. Lillian was born in February 1947. Her birth father married another woman that same month.

Lillian's feelings about Georgia Tann are conflicted, and I sit on the edge of the sofa and lean forward to hear what she will say. "I'm sure she did some good," she admits. And yet Lillian knows she came close to dying in Tann's care. It's a heavy realization to handle. Dealing with the past and the challenges of life, she admits, makes her blue at times. Still, she realizes that her life is much better because of her adoption. "When you take a step back and look, I've been so blessed." She considers trying one of the popular inexpensive DNA tests to find more family connections. But she doubts that she will. "It's not a driving force in my life. I can't get all excited about the family who gave me away."

She and Joyce continue to meet for low-key visits. "Slowly, slowly we are forging a relationship," Lillian says. "We've gotten to be friends." She smiles, at peace with her life in this moment. "I was an only child until age fifty, and now I have two half sisters."

DO THE RIGHT THING

———

*T*he city has grown up around Lillian's home, her quiet street close to the hubbub of modern Memphis. I ease out onto a thoroughfare with our visit still on my mind. She spent years pouring herself into students in her classroom and her own children and grandchildren, and now she's navigating the world as a widow. Yet she marches on, a diligent crusader of sorts, on a quest to see what comes next. She plans to join us for the reunion, but she is helping administer an ACT test that Saturday morning and isn't sure how late she will arrive.

Another reminder of the short time frame on which this gathering is balanced. That people have other plans. Responsibilities. They're busy.

And yet Lillian welcomed me into her day, prepared a space for me with flowers from the garden and homemade cake on a china plate. Gave me the gift of time—the rarest and most precious commodity in today's overcommitted world.

Do I make strangers as welcome in my life as this woman has made me in hers?

The thought whips me into a grocery store parking lot to try to fix a reunion snag I've discovered. When I ducked into the gathering room at our hotel earlier, I was disappointed to find that it was Sterile . . . with a capital *S*. Unwelcoming and unhospitable.

I grab a basket, then hesitate. Is this premature? I have no idea how many people to buy for. What would they like? Wine! People like wine, right? But red or white? How about chocolate! Who doesn't like chocolate? Maybe bottled water for non-wine drinkers. And chips. Napkins. And fresh flowers. I grab items as if we're hosting a wedding reception for two hundred, think of Lillian, and push aside my doubts.

It's not hard knowing where she got her kind heart. I can almost see her adoptive father moving across the room where, as a newborn, she lay dying.

Never hesitate. Do the right thing.

Now, that's a lesson to take with us.

I head to the cash register. If these groceries bring strangers together in even the smallest way, they will be worth the effort. If the reunion opens even one happy door for an adoptee or leads to the discovery of important family information, it will be the right thing.

Pushing the cart back to the car, I'm eager to show Lisa and our adoptee-coordinator, Connie, what I've bought.

CHAPTER 11

REUNION EVE

"All you can do is jump in and see where it goes."

THE DUSTY WINGATE FAMILY CAR PULLS INTO THE HOTEL'S covered drive, and Lisa hops out in a summer-print sundress and sandals. She looks only slightly road-weary after criss-crossing Arkansas in a government van with a kindly state librarian, visiting a dozen libraries.

My relief that she has actually made it is ridiculously high, my nerves on edge because her final stop on the Arkansas book tour was only hours before. Many things had to fall into place for us both to be at this hotel at this moment. To meet the logistical challenge of getting her from rural Arkansas to Memphis required her husband, Sam, driving from Texas to her mother's home in the Ozark Mountains to drop off their dog-child, Huckleberry, then to southeast Arkansas to pick Lisa up and deliver her to the reunion. My tense arms are waiting to give both of them a hug.

"Yay!" Lisa sings out with her usual big smile. "We're here. We made it!"

A trace of pre-party jitters dances around Lisa's face but doesn't distract her from plunging right into the lobby and the reunion weekend ahead. One way or another, this thing is happening. At least now we have flowers. And wine. And chocolate. Enough to welcome everyone if only a small group shows. Enough to welcome everyone if a *large* group shows. Friendships, we hope, will be forged. Stories will be told and preserved.

Here. In Memphis. Where the plot of *Before We Were Yours* took shape. Where, for decades, Georgia Tann altered lives on a whim.

Where one year ago this very week, Lisa chose to introduce the novel to the world at the Memphis Public Libraries' summer reading kickoff event.

The venues have changed so many times that it's only with the help of a timetable emailed today from Lisa's mother that we think we *might* know where we are supposed to be and when. Another round of events has been scheduled, filled, and then expanded to include a book talk and an informal supper at Kirby Pines Retirement Community; a Saturday gathering at the library for anyone with connections to TCHS; a book talk at Novel bookstore, owned and operated by Memphis residents in a lovely neighborhood; a visit to the cemetery monument in honor of children who died in Tann's care; and two Sunday afternoon talks in the Elmwood Cemetery chapel.

This packed agenda has come together with Scotch tape and crossed fingers, more nebulous than either of us would prefer. We're fairly sure we've made adoptee-organizer Connie and the hotel staff crazy more than once with rotating hospitality suites, ever-changing blocks of rooms, and imprecise guest lists.

The weekend is shaping up to be a cross between a happy family reunion and a small high school homecoming—with plenty of talking, listening, and updates on who was found and how. Even now, just a night's sleep away from the first event, Lisa and I confess to each other that we are depending heavily on the kindness of strangers and the blessings of good people.

Some adoptees' participation remains iffy, whether because of surgery, distance, or doubt. Sadly, Patricia lets us know for sure that health concerns will prevent her from being here. It's a blow to lose one of the core group, but we'll FaceTime her into the gatherings.

We're thrilled with the expected adoptees and their family members who we're sure will take part. Plus, there are some new people Lisa met at various Arkansas book events. She hopes several will join us on the spur of the moment, and we pencil their names in on our messy spreadsheet.

These include Robert Terrell, a businessman adopted for seven dollars and delivered to the back door of a rural Arkansas house—giving him a life he insists he would not change. And his daughter Heather Spencer who wants to know her family's medical history and more about what is hidden.

And Stanley Henderson, who is still, in his early seventies, searching for a brother the family believes was stolen by Georgia Tann. He told the story to Lisa only days ago, on the last stop of her Arkansas tour. He was tentative and intense about his infant brother, in tears as he described what happened.

The encounters in neighboring Arkansas bolster Lisa's expectations for the weekend. For me, most of the names represent strangers on a quest for information or restoration, and I cannot wait to hear their stories in their words.

Another lifelong Arkansan will also join us this weekend: my first cousin Cindy Self, retired from mail carrying in the Mississippi Delta and a passionate professional photographer.

In our childhood, she roped me into getting on the back of a horse with her and flying over ditches on her family farm, and shamed me into jumping off river bluffs into murky water.

This weekend I have roped *her* into photographing and videoing events and individuals with the promise of little pay, a free hotel room, and sandwiches on the run—along with a plea for maximum flexibility. "Have I mentioned that we do not exactly know what will happen and when?" I ask her. *A photographer's nightmare.* Her husband, Doug, a retired U.S. Coast Guard officer, will join her, holding cameras and lighting equipment and patiently driving her to Elmwood Cemetery a day early to check out the morning light. Meanwhile, I'll be using our conference room and my hotel suite to do interviews with various attendees.

Unexpectedly, the publisher of *Before We Were Yours* has also assigned a video crew to capture this historic occasion. The crew will arrive on Saturday for interviews and meet us at the cemetery Sunday morning to visit the TCHS memorial marker. That adds another layer of logistics and hatches a few more butterflies.

As we mill around the hotel, we discover a flaw in the agenda: no official kickoff has been planned. *Why didn't we think of a registration area to say hello?* Instead, we will simply dive into our group activities tomorrow, starting with a large afternoon gathering for the public at Kirby Pines, with the hope that we will meet reunion-goers there, not knowing who will show or if they will want to speak up.

"All you can do is jump in and see where it goes," Lisa said a few days ago.

Connie, whom we only know through the email that brought us to this moment and the harried chats that followed, is the first adoptee to arrive, and hers will be the first reunion interview I do. She is such an integral part of the weekend, and I know that her story will be one of both heartache and resilience. Lisa and I each let out a breath when we see her smiling face.

Then we all jump off the cliff together.

CHAPTER 12

THE ONLY HOME
SHE KNOWS

———

"We've been looking for you for forty years."

T HE YOUNG MOTHER AND SOLDIER FATHER ARE THE PARENTS of a three-year-old son, but their home is far from stable and secure.

As is the case with many young men in the 1940s, the father returns from military action with more than souvenirs from the other side of the world. He brings a condition then called battle fatigue or shell shock. Not until years later will it be known as post-traumatic stress disorder. The couple divorces not long after the soldier's return.

The wife, Lydia Marie, is educated and from a well-off family, but most women in this era are encouraged to find a husband rather than a job. Although she becomes engaged to another man, her new relationship is complicated. Likely still drawn to the love of her past, Lydia falls into a short affair, rumored to be with her ex-husband. Still, she marries her fiancé, Arthur Dillard, hoping to form a new family for herself and her preschool-age son.

But turmoil soon breaks out. She is pregnant, and, given the timing, her new husband claims he is not the father of the baby.

Furious and unwilling to accept yet another stepchild, he contacts the Tennessee Children's Home Society to arrange for the baby to be given away or sold. He even makes plans to pay for a worker to pick the newborn up when the time comes. To hide the pregnancy from family and neighbors, the errant bride is shipped out of state to deliver the baby in secret and be done with it. The practice is not uncommon, though most such mothers-to-be are unmarried.

Tiny Mary Joan, born in July 1950, is taken from her mother when she is a week old. In the arms of a Tann helper, the infant travels to Memphis. A bassinet at the Main Receiving Home awaits, a holding space that won't be needed for long. Tann's plans for this fair-haired newborn have long been in the works, and they are about to come to fruition.

The new parents, Janice and Roy Wilson, arrive to pick up their daughter with a load of their own baggage. Other agencies have turned them down. At ages forty and forty-two, they are too old for a conventional adoption and are dealing with an emotional crisis. Janice is severely depressed over the recent crib death of their six-month-old child.

They know that a baby can be procured through Georgia Tann. Quickly.

They have the money to make the arrangements.

They pick up Mary Joan and drive to their home on the other side of Memphis. She will spend the first ten years of her life in this city, her name changed to Connie Christine. They pay Tann approximately seven hundred fifty dollars, well beyond the legal price of a standard adoption.

Janice and Roy, with all of their flaws, become baby Connie's true mom and dad. She also gains an eleven-year-old sister, Shelly, who becomes the love of her life, a constant in a sea of uncertainty. A caseworker's report later notes that Shelly seems to feel that Connie is especially hers, mothering her and making over her. "She actually does more for her than Janice does," the worker writes. "Connie, on the other hand, seems to be just as crazy about Shelly."

The couple is eager to repair their family. This tiny baby, like so many of Tann's charges, arrives in her new home with a job to do. A problem to fix.

The repairs this couple needs are more than any child could handle.

Connie

A RETIREE WITH MULTIPLE HOMES, A LARGE GROUP OF FRIENDS, and a precious dog, Connie has a full life—but a TCHS-sized gap remains in her heart. Her commitment to bringing adoptees together reflects her need to meet others like her, to help them, and to grow from the experience.

She enters a room with the presence of a woman who knows what she wants—but her confidence conceals how deeply affected she still is by the circumstances that brought her into the world in July 1950. And the turmoil that followed.

When Connie and I meet in the hotel lobby, she has flown in from the West Coast on a red-eye and hopped out of bed before dawn to appear on a morning Memphis television program with Lisa. And she looks wonderful. She appears younger than I expected, an attractive woman with stylish blond hair and tanned skin. Her clothes are resort casual. Although we have spoken on the phone and emailed to prepare for this visit, we approach each other as curious strangers. Outgoing and yet cautious, she suggests that we meet for lunch at a nearby restaurant to do our interview. We'll have a couple of hours before we head back to the hotel for more work on the weekend's logistics.

At the restaurant, she chats up the waiter and listens intently to his story. Her smile is engaging. When Connie was a toddler, a social worker came to the Wilsons' home to do an assessment before the adoption was finalized. The worker gushed about the toddler's personality, looks, and intelligence. As Connie talks, those traits, weathered somewhat by decades of pain and uncertainty, still shine. But a fear of abandonment, a need for approval, and a life spent as an overachiever fill her story. She has struggled to please anyone and everyone and to somehow find her place. She tells me, "I just felt different. You don't fit . . . and people don't understand."

A life built on other people's secrets brings that on.

"I always knew I was adopted," she continues. "I was told my biological parents had been killed in a car accident."

Janice, her adoptive mother, comes from a wealthy family in Washington, D.C. Her great-grandfather was President Abraham Lincoln's bodyguard. "Though not," Connie informs me with a smile, "on duty the day Lincoln was killed."

Roy, her adoptive father, owns a struggling plumbing business, then takes a job as a plumbing salesman.

Connie has barely landed in their arms before the cracks in their relationship widen. They argue over money, and their baby suffers again from a mother's indiscretion. "My mom ended up having an affair during the adoption process," she says.

Only two months old when the public scandal about TCHS erupts, Connie has secured her place as one of the youngest of the TCHS adoptees. No more children will be subjected to a Tann adoption. The TCHS Memphis orphanage is shut down. Over the coming months, child welfare workers are sent to the homes of those awaiting finalized adoptions, making assessments of where children have been placed. For Connie, the visit comes when she is twenty-two months old. A detailed report to a judge paints a picture of a tumultuous home but leaves no doubt that Connie is an exceptionally bright and pretty child:

> Although this is a house which we would never have selected for placement of a child, we feel that since Connie has been there since she was two weeks old and this is the only home that she knows, and her development has been good, it would be to the child's best interest to allow the adoption to be consummated.

From a caseworker's notes about Connie: "She is a very pleasant child and plays all the time and seldom cries."

As soon as the adoption is final, Janice remarries—and, once more, Connie finds herself in a situation where the new husband doesn't want the children. Over the next few years, Connie and her older sister, Shelly, who has taken on the role of mother, are tossed around among relatives. When Connie's adoptive father, Roy, remarries, more heartbreak follows. "I loved my daddy so much," she says. "I was the apple of his eye." But at age six, after witnessing a fight between her dad and her stepmom, she grabs a paper bag, puts her PJs in it, goes into another room to call a taxi, and heads to her mother's house. In her precocious way, she tells them, "I can't live like this anymore."

Janice is deeply in love with her current husband, but she is guilt-ridden over abandoning her daughters and leaves him so she can keep Connie and Shelly. She eventually remarries yet again. "Dad married two women. Mom married four men," Connie says. "And then they finally got back together."

At her home in California, Connie keeps a photograph of herself and her dad, Roy, on her desk, a casual shot taken at a fair in Memphis when she was seven. She also displays a photo of the couple, who, in spite of everything, and flawed though they might have been, will always be her parents.

A hard worker, Connie starts her first job at age fourteen; she works every summer and after school, struggling to pay expenses in her uncertain life. At nineteen, she becomes a flight attendant, moving into management by her early twenties. She does not take vacations or go out to eat. Unlike some TCHS adoptees, Connie does not fantasize about her birth parents. "I was so busy trying to survive," she says. "I always had to save every single penny because I didn't want to be poor ever again . . . I never thought I would have anything permanent in my life. I got those survival skills way back then." She moves from place to place, never having a real home.

Even while listening to Connie tell me about her successful career, I sense the underlying melancholy she feels about her young years. She sighs. "I always knew I didn't fit. I was super

Connie, one of the last adoptees from the Tennessee Children's Home Society in Memphis, and her adoptive father at the Memphis Fair in 1957.

hyper. My IQ tests were very high." Her voice turns pensive. "I never did get to college." In young adulthood, tragedy leads to a new sense of urgency. When she is twenty-four, her adoptive mother dies. When she is twenty-nine, her husband of five years dies of a heart attack while playing tennis. A year to the day later, her adoptive father dies. With Janice and Roy gone, her older sister, Shelly, reveals family secrets about Connie's adoption through TCHS and contradicts the story Connie has been told. Her birth parents were not killed in a car wreck; the story is messier.

Connie's desire to know her birth-family history escalates.

A niece dies shortly after this, followed by the death of Shelly, the sister Connie calls her rock. "You learn how to survive, and you don't let the little things get to you," she says. "You know you'll get through anything, pretty much. You also learn not to stay in bad situations, and you learn how to take care of yourself." During this difficult period, she strengthens herself through therapy. "I have sought counseling off and on my entire life," she says.

Her therapist is the one who pushes her to work on her deeper issues. "Your real problem is your adoption," she tells Connie. "You've carried pain with you your whole life."

Connie has no way to know it yet, but the pain and loss that began when she was adopted are not only hers. In a nearby city, and yet a world away, her birth mother, Lydia, battles the torment of having given her daughter up. She struggles with questions that linger when a mother sends a child into the world with no further contact. When Lydia remarries, she does not tell her husband about her brief second marriage, or the daughter she surrendered. At holidays, Connie will learn much later, her biological mother voices veiled guilt to family members.

"You just don't know what I've done," she would say.

THE DEATHS OF SO many close to Connie forge a strong desire within her to learn her medical history, but frustration follows. Her voice is tinged with anger as she discusses it: "I couldn't find any of my records ... It wasn't that I was looking for a family, but I really wanted to know if I had cancer in my blood or heart disease in my genetics."

Then she sees a news program about TCHS.

"*Sixty Minutes* is how I found my family," she says. Through the program in the early 1990s, she learns of a woman named Denny Glad, who embarked on a mission to help TCHS adoptees find their birth families. While the state's adoption records were still under lock and key, unavailable to those searching for their hidden pasts, Denny traveled to courthouses throughout Tennessee with a cadre of volunteers; they tediously sifted through years of public court dockets to compile information not easily available to adoptees. Along the way, she was reportedly offered access to the records of a judge who had died, and, through these, she found more names of Tann children. Denny and others meticulously recorded names and dates on index cards, a pre-Internet system that made information accessible when adoptees turned to her for help. She eventually successfully crusaded to have the state's adoption records opened.

After seeing the TV show, Connie makes contact with Denny, and it is this remarkable advocate who finds accurate information about Connie's past. When Connie opens the package of information that arrives at her home on her fortieth birthday, she learns, as she feared, that her biological mother died young.

But not from an illness. She choked on a piece of meat at age fifty. Connie will never meet her.

The records lead Connie to another relative, an aunt in Mississippi, her mother's sister—the companion who lived out of state with Connie's mother during the birth. "I finally mustered the courage to call her sister, who held me at birth and knew exactly who I was," Connie says.

When they speak, the aunt's words are beautiful and yet devastating: "Honey, let me stop you right there. We've been looking for you for forty years."

Connie's aunt tells her that her birth grandparents, who lived in Tennessee, took apples to the orphanage for the children living there for years after Connie was given up. In a gut-wrenching twist, she learns that her birth mother had moved to the Northeast, close to Connie's home as an adult. Her brother, Graham, just a toddler all those years ago when her mother fled to give birth in secrecy, also lived not far from her. But the family reconnection will be rocky. "We can't tell your brother," the aunt says. "No one knows except me."

Finally, the aunt tells her son, Wes, who as a preschooler had also been with them at the time of Connie's birth. Wes insists that Connie's brother, Graham, be told. Connie reunites with Graham in the early 1990s while she's in New York City for a job interview. He is also headed into the city, and they meet at six o'clock at the iconic Rainbow Room. "He walked in the door and I knew immediately it was my brother. I'd never seen anyone who looked like me. When I met my brother, it was like a tiny piece of a jigsaw puzzle."

The similarities are uncanny. "It was wonderful and yet surreal to finally see someone who looked like me, who *was* like me. We shared similar physical qualities, the same ethics, similar taste in music, wine, sports, and countless other things. He'd grown up on the East Coast and I on the West Coast." Although geography separated their upbringing, they landed in the same region in middle adulthood and are much alike in temperament as well, happy and energetic. Their relationship gels with his advice about the job she's going for. "He is always like a big brother and helps me make life decisions," she says. "Rumor has it that I have the same father as my brother. Who knows? We have never done the DNA."

She and her aunt also get to know each other. "She had a huge family reunion when it was no longer a secret," Connie says. "Ultimately, we had a very good relationship." She gushes about members of her birth family, but like many adoptees, those relationships bear the wounds of lives long separated. She and Graham stay in touch; because they live once more on different coasts, however, they do not see each other regularly. Now Connie hangs on to dear friends, including a group from her junior high days. She mourns girlfriends who are starting to pass away. Although she dates regularly, she has no plans to remarry. "I never think anything's going to last," she says.

A fresh blessing for her are new friendships with the TCHS adoptees with whom she's been communicating via email. Within the next twenty-four hours, she'll meet some of them in person. "Even across the miles that separate us, there's an unexplainable sense of sisterhood," she says, "and a strange sense of comfort at no longer feeling like 'the only one.'"

OPEN AND CLOSED

————

*N*ot everyone is as prepared as Connie to talk about their life experiences and lessons learned. This is a truth I've discovered in the weeks before our reunion weekend.

In the course of the many phone interviews and the hastily arranged visits I've undertaken during the past couple of months, I've had lovely meetings with people who decided, after privately opening the book of their lives to me, that they'd just as soon not make their stories public.

I've chatted with a smart, witty woman in her seventies and her elegant, soft-spoken adoptive mother, who's more than one hundred years old. The mother described loving her infant daughter from the first time she laid eyes on her, but she is not eager to talk much more about the adoption. Although the daughter has searched and found some answers to her biological family background, there's a lifetime of water under that bridge. Too many people are involved, too many lives affected. It's all better kept among family.

Others share snippets of information. A son reads *Before We Were Yours* and reaches out to tell us that his mother, who was not Jewish, was sent from TCHS to a Jewish couple in the Midwest. When her siblings located her, decades later, he encouraged her to connect with them and flew home for the celebration. Walking into the house where he grew up, he thought he saw his mother in the hall, her back to him. When she turned, he was not looking at his mother. He was seeing his aunt, his mother's birth sister. Life had changed. But he's a busy executive at a nonprofit organization and ultimately does not wish to tell his story publicly.

At times, adult children of adoptees are the ones reopening the family history book, seeking answers. Two daughters have signed up to bring fathers to the reunion because they want to know more. And they believe that the journey will help their dads. Two more talk to me about their fathers' stories over the phone. Another man calls me to discuss his mother's past.

Open book. Closed book. Seeking truth is an individual choice, one that everyone, adopted or not, makes at some point in their lives. Each of us creates our own life story, the one we tell ourselves and others. Or choose not to tell.

As I hustle to leave for our first official reunion event—the Friday afternoon public book talk hosted by Kirby Pines Retirement Community—I realize that this is what we're doing this weekend: writing a story in which we have no idea how each chapter will fit. The results may well be mixed. With celebration there may also come barriers, and a reluctance to dig deeper, toward the truth.

When we meet up in the lobby of the retirement community, Lisa and I give each other a brief pep talk, and then we stride up the gorgeous spiral staircase to the second floor and into the large and well-appointed auditorium. The room is packed with Kirby Pines residents, members of the public, and folks with connections to TCHS. Because of our epic fail on planning a meet-and-greet reunion event, we have no way of knowing who's who. We happily spot Connie coming in with two other core group members. That's three of them, at least.

Then I see Lillian, whom I interviewed soon after arriving in Memphis. I give her a hug and have the pleasure of introducing Lisa to her.

Four. That's four of them who can get to know one another, anyway.

Why didn't we think to reserve a row for TCHS attendees up front, to be sure they could get a seat?

Too late now.

My cousin Cindy is snapping pictures everywhere; her husband, Doug, is fastening a camera on a tripod. My husband, Paul, and Lisa's husband, Sam, are on hand as well, serving this weekend as drivers, waiters, and unofficial jacks-of-all-trades.

The room buzzes with anticipation . . . or is that just our nerves?

————

As Lisa speaks from the front, I scan the crowd, trying to pick out adoptee James Sanders and his wife and daughter. We are to sit down for an interview after this event, then join other adoptees for dinner in the Kirby Pines cafeteria.

Did their flight from Utah make it?

I have no way of knowing. He could, like every other TCHS adoptee, be any face in the crowd.

CHAPTER 13

HANDED OFF IN A TRAIN STATION

*"We found both sides of my family.
I'm meeting them Sunday and Monday."*

IN APRIL 1944, MARJORIE HABLET, TWENTY-TWO AND unmarried, travels from Arkansas to Memphis to give birth to a premature boy.

He's tiny, just four pounds.

She favors her son with a name that signifies strength, importance. Marcus Walter, after the baby's father and her brother. She has, at least in that moment, intentions for this infant. Hopes.

Yet little Marcus winds up in the hands of the Tennessee Children's Home Society. Only a month old, he is transported from Tennessee to California and dropped into the eager arms of his new parents at three A.M. at Grand Central Station in Los Angeles.

Iris and Charlie Sanders are neighbors of famous Hollywood cowboy Smiley Burnette, who told the eager couple about adopting children from TCHS. As soon as baby Marcus is handed off, the female escort from the orphanage vanishes.

James

ON A THURSDAY IN JUNE, JAMES SANDERS BOARDS A PLANE TO fly from warm, dry Salt Lake City to warmer, humid Memphis. His wife and daughter stay close by his side, both excited about the trip.

But James, seventy-four when he makes his return sojourn to Memphis, is not sure he wants to be back here in this city he has not visited since birth. He's about to open a door that can't be closed again. No telling what might be on the other side. When they arrive, an Uber driver picks them up. It's after midnight.

"You guys are sure coming in late," the driver remarks. "What are you here for?"

They chuckle. "Long story short?" James quips.

But he does not have a quick reply. How can one easily explain a suspicious adoption, a lifetime of wondering, a search that has led to mounds of information on Georgia Tann and TCHS, and a planned blood-family meeting—one he thought he might never have?

His daughter, Brigette, has located James's biological family. On this trip to attend the TCHS reunion, he will not only meet other survivors, he will travel to meet relatives who live just over the Mississippi border from Memphis. He hopes to connect with other family members near Little Rock, Arkansas. He would be highly pleased to meet his half brothers, although they have not responded to inquiries. He has lunch plans with his birth mother's step-grandchildren, adults with memories of the mama he never knew.

The plans thrill him but also have him slightly worked up. *Will these meetings occur? What will the mood of his "new" family be? Will their gathering be awkward? Comfortable? Will he be welcomed or held at arm's length?*

These upcoming family meetings are as hard to predict as it is for Lisa and me to envision this weekend's gathering. There are way too many unknowns.

The Sanders family heard about this event only a few weeks ago, after Brigette reached out to Lisa about her father's story and the connection she felt to the families in *Before We Were Yours*. Since then, they've booked flights, made hotel reservations, contacted the blood relatives Brigette found, planned get-togethers, and traveled halfway across the country.

After a too-short night's sleep, they join the crowd in the auditorium of Kirby Pines to attend the first event on the schedule, a book talk. They've been told that other adoptees and family members will be there, and in the sea of faces, they wonder who was once traded off by Tann. Or who has personal memories of the scandal. This *is* Memphis, after all. The scandal was front-page news here. It was also back-room gossip.

As the book talk begins, Lisa shares the history of the scandal that inspired her novel. She speaks about coming across the true story by accident, about wanting to know more, *needing* to know more, wondering why she'd never heard of Georgia Tann.

She explains about doing research, about contemplating how to tell the story as a novel. Although the scandal has, over the years, received coverage on talk shows, in news stories, and in a handful of nonfiction books, she says, "I realized that what had not been told were the stories of these ordinary children. What was it like to be taken from your life, with no explanation, and dropped into another one?"

She pauses to look out over the crowd for a moment, then reads from the novel: *"The river is ours. It is only ours."* Lisa looks up at her audience. "The characters are always real in my head. While writing these stories, I traveled through the journey with these kids. I wanted their story to reflect the stories of the real-life survivors." She shares information about this week-end's planned reunion and thanks Kirby Pines for inviting adoptees to have dinner together tonight in their dining room—an invaluable get-to-know-you opportunity for the TCHS group, people who've met long-distance, if at all.

Although Lisa is the only scheduled speaker this afternoon, she whets an appetite for more. A few of the adoptees and fam-ily members have spoken up from their chairs... and the crowd's interest is piqued. When hostess Janice announces a break during the Q&A so that the punch and cookies at the back of the room will not go untasted, she invites the TCHS adoptees to move up front and join in. *Perhaps they'd like to share a bit of their own stories, answer questions, give their thoughts?*

The moment isn't planned, but the invitation is open. It hangs in the air, expectant. An opportunity.

A reserved and generally quiet man, James has seated him-self near the back of the auditorium with his wife and daughter. Brigette doesn't think he'll want to speak.

When the time comes, though, James stands and haltingly makes his way to the front, a shy look on his face. His wife of forty-seven years, Millie, a lovely woman with a happy smile, stands, too. Brigette, in her late thirties, walks up the aisle, a few steps behind her father, in case she's needed, then takes a seat to the side with her mother.

James sits with other adoptees behind a folding table and weeps as he shares his history with the audience, his soft voice even quieter than usual as he says, "My parents paid twelve hundred dollars."

His is an unlikely Hollywood story, filled with the twists

and turns of an action movie, the pathos of a drama, and the love story of a romance. He is a most appealing character—gentle, positive, and insightful, with a family that adores him in a way that shows he is a very good father. That's part of the reason he's here. He hesitated at first about coming. Brigette told him he needed to.

"I just didn't want to come back here, but Brigette insisted," he quips with a laugh. "When Brigette tells you to do something, you have to do it."

His heartfelt words and his evident love for his daughter delight the audience. After he and the other adoptees finish telling their stories—such an unexpected and emotional scene—James chats with his new fans. Then, escaping the chaos of the crowded room, he sinks onto a sofa in a well-appointed reception area, so that he and I can visit one-on-one.

We are all still surprised by the stories that were just offered up by the adoptees. James, his eyes moist behind his glasses, seems a bit overwhelmed—or maybe I am the one overwhelmed. We chat for a few minutes to regain our bearings. Wife Millie sits nearby, content to listen and give moral support. Brigette, her brown hair brushing against her shoulders, holds a large notebook of materials she has gathered through the years. She is the keeper of the records but encourages her dad to tell the story.

THE DATE IS MAY 16, 1944, when Marcus, still a small thing, arrives in California at the home of his new parents. His adoptive dad, Charlie, is a procurement officer for the Navy, and his mother, Iris, is a social worker. They give him another strong name: James, with the middle name of Glennan, in honor of the man who will become the first administrator of the National

Aeronautics and Space Administration. This baby is wanted, and his life seems promising.

Baby James. It turns out he shares his birth name with a newly discovered cousin but is only now piecing together the story of his heritage.

But the golden California dream does not materialize for James and his adoptive parents.

First, a foreboding typewritten letter from Tann, addressed to Iris and Charlie, arrives in January 1945. The letter hints at the scandal that James's new parents know nothing of.

"We are taking this opportunity to advise you that we are anticipating some changes in our Tennessee Adoption laws, which will no doubt go into effect after the adjournment of our Legislature, now in session," it reads. "We feel that it might be advisable for those with children in their homes not yet adopted to complete these adoptions at an early date."

The letter then outlines options for a worker to visit and help finalize the adoption, as long as James's parents are "fully satisfied that the child now in your home is the one for you," with payment to be made directly to Tann. "Kindly let us hear from you immediately, via AIR MAIL, if you wish to have our worker see you as outlined above, making your check payable to Miss Georgia Tann and mark same 'For transportation and court costs.'"

Adoption stress mixes with home problems. When the war ends, Charlie takes a Navy position in the Oakland area, but Iris does not want to move from Southern California. Charlie travels back and forth for a while; when James is about three, however, he hears his parents arguing. After that, his mother tells him his dad has left—and that he is adopted.

His parents soon divorce, leaving him once again without a father. "It's a very interesting thing, not having a dad," James says.

The small ranch home where James and his mother live has two extra bedrooms, and Iris takes in veterans being treated at a nearby hospital. At night, James sometimes hears them screaming—because, his mother explains, of injuries they suffered in the war.

On the occasions when his adoptive mother cannot take care of him, her mother steps in. "I had a wonderful, wonderful grandmother . . . She was just an amazing woman." An example of how one person can make such a difference in a life, she becomes his biggest supporter and takes him regularly to the Methodist church, where her elderly friends love him. "Those ladies took good care of me." Affection flows in his words. "I never got whipped or spanked." An avid baseball fan, his grandmother uses her love of the game to help him when he struggles with math as a youngster, walking with him to minor-league baseball games and teaching him arithmetic by counting the twelve blocks to and from the field. "In all honesty," James says, "I was blessed."

Even so, a long period of relocating around California follows for James and his mother. They live in seventeen homes and he attends eight schools, never quite sure where he will be for his next grade. The character of Rill in *Before We Were Yours* reminds him of his eleven-year-old self. At that age, James had a seven-days-a-week paper route, serving forty-four houses. He made five dollars a month. The income was something steady in an often unstable world.

When James is about twelve, Iris becomes an alcoholic. "I grew up in a bar in Pasadena, California," he says. He is not joking. In a homemade video, he recalls his life at the tavern with his mother and eating his favorite supper—two hard-boiled eggs, Fritos, and an orange soda. Sometimes he falls asleep while his mother drinks. Many nights, he awakens in a stranger's home with his mother, who is sobering up. He is not quite sure how they made it through those times, but he is reluctant to speak ill of Iris.

He measures his words when he reflects on his life with his adoptive mother. His considerate spirit shines. "My mom, when she wasn't drunk, was a very good mom. My mom loved me. My grandmother loved me." His birth family, as far as he knew, had abandoned him. "I figured, Well, they didn't want me, so here I am."

The chaotic childhood marks James, but it does not defeat him. If anything, it leaves him resourceful, determined, appreciative.

In high school, he discovers pole vaulting and buys a piece of bamboo for fifty cents from a rug company for his first pole. His success at the sport improves his confidence and encourages him to stretch in other areas of his life, from making friends to taking harder classes.

He chooses to attend Brigham Young University, in part because it is a school that doesn't allow alcohol; while there, he is baptized into the Church of Jesus Christ of Latter Day Saints.

He then goes into the Army as a Special Forces medic in Vietnam. Upon his return, he is in the first physician's assistant class at the University of Utah and has a long career in that field.

Now retired, James is dealing with health issues from Vietnam, where he was exposed to Agent Orange. He has had two small strokes and triple-bypass surgery. He suffers from diabetes and had to have the toes on one foot amputated, so now he depends on a cane. The health problems have not, however, cooled his desire to solve the mysteries of his biological history. When he was in his thirties, about the age of his daughter, Brigette, now, he began to search. He is quick to emphasize, however, that his adoptive mother will always be his mom, and he stresses his love for Charlie and Iris with a soft but impassioned voice. They did not know anything about the Tann scandal before the news broke, or even for years afterward. Preoccupied with the chaos of their lives, they were oblivious.

In the 1980s, before Tennessee adoption records are opened, James connects with a woman who has been successful in tracking down her own biological sisters, who were Tann babies from Memphis. She tells James she has a good friend who is a nurse at the hospital where James was born. For fifty dollars, the friend can get hospital microfiche records for him. He pays and gets some information. The nurse is not the only one operating a sort of cottage industry during this period, taking in a little cash while helping TCHS babies find their birth families, particularly before the Internet becomes more widely used.

Later, James turns to the state of Tennessee, which costs him more money. The word from them? "Your mother has died, and that's that." But a report on a CBS television program changes his perspective, with word that perhaps there *is* more information available for TCHS adoptees. James writes to the network, and an assistant there tells him whom to contact.

James, Brigette, and a genealogist neighbor, Linda, persist in the search. Linda, who does genealogy research at James's church, encourages him to find out what he can. At first James does not have enough information—and what he has is vague. Finally, he finds the names of his birth mother and father and their ages. That is enough for Linda to go on. "He gave me several clues that really opened it up for me," she tells me on the telephone. "It just started flowing . . . Doors were opening after so many years. He didn't give up hope."

Linda checks census records and begins to feel secure about the family research. She uses FamilySearch.org, Ancestry.com, and sometimes Google. One of the first things she examines is FindAGrave.com. "You receive a world of information if you can get into the cemetery records." As she draws the pieces together, it's thrilling. "I knew how much it meant to him . . . It's like having a mystery so long and having it solved. I loved every minute of it. I felt like I was an investigator. James is kind of a quiet person, but he's been excited to share his journey. Other people have been thrilled for him."

Brigette has used the information from Linda and her own research to dive deeper for details of her dad's heritage. "If you need someone to dig under the rocks, Brigette's the one," James says.

"It's like working a puzzle or unraveling a mystery," Brigette explains as we sit together, enjoying the respite after the emotional gathering in the auditorium.

They go on to fill me in about James's adoptive father, Charlie, a missing player in the story of James's childhood, the man who left and did not come back—for decades. James's adoptive mother, Iris, who never remarries, tells James that his father has died. So imagine their surprise when twelve-year-old Brigette answers the phone and Charlie is on the other end.

After he identifies himself as her grandfather, she is confused and hands the phone to her mother, who asks a few questions and informs a stunned James who is on the phone. "He has all the right answers," Millie tells James.

Charlie comes to visit, and James meets him at the airport, unsure of what to say or do. He watches his father, equally unsure, exit the plane. "I walked up to him and said, 'Dad, it's James,' and he started crying."

Past hurts are forgiven, and they develop a good relationship. Charlie had four children with his second wife, and although Charlie is now dead, his family maintains a connection with their adopted brother. "His kids are really good to us," James says.

We pause on this sweet story. The staff of Kirby Pines has our table all set up in the dining room—maybe we can talk more over dinner. We definitely want to hear the details about another reunion ahead for James. He is scheduled to visit, for the first time, several relatives uncovered by recent sleuthing.

He has Brigette to thank for that. Brigette, who is part caretaker, part detective, and all daughter. Watching her walk slowly beside James through the halls of Kirby Pines, her carefully organized family research notebook tucked under one arm, it's easy to see she's awfully good at all three roles.

POINTS OF INTEREST

*B*etween the reunion events in Memphis, Brigette has an agenda planned for their visit. She has carefully mapped various sites that are part of her father's early life and drives her parents to each of them. One is the former location of John Gaston Hospital, which has since been torn down. "Well, Dad, this is where you were born," she says.

Mom Millie lightens the moment when she points to the medical center now on the site. "Oh, there's the Elvis Presley Emergency Room."

The three then go to where Tann's orphanage stood on Poplar Avenue. The turn-of-the-century mansion is long gone. A commercial building stands in its place. Together, father, mother, and daughter walk across the big lawn out back. Memphis lore holds that some babies who perished in the orphanage were buried there, but I cannot find any information to verify that. "We were kind of wondering if there are still little bodies out there," James says. "It was a very sad deal."

They also visit the cemetery memorial to babies who died in the care of TCHS. "That was emotional. It really was," James says. "I was thinking about Lisa's book." He recalled how the book's cover does not show the faces of the two children. For the children buried at Elmwood, he says, "You never got to see who they were."

For James, at least some of the mysteries will be solved over the course of this weekend. When he, Millie, and Brigette depart Memphis, they will drive to Little Rock, Arkansas, to meet other family members.

They will not, though, be seeing James's half brothers, whose names Brigette found through an obituary. "I wrote them this letter. 'This is my Dad; we don't want anything.' Neither of them responded." The regret in those words is unmistakable. She can only hope that the rest of the meetings with James's biological cousins will go as planned. So much hope has been invested in this trip, so much effort, so many years of searching. She wants it to be great. As great as her dad, who deserves this.

Wouldn't it be wonderful if the phone would ring, and her father would get the chance to meet his half brothers, after all? "It's a shock to many people. We're hoping that their hearts will be softened, and they will want to meet my father, too," Brigette says. "We shall see."

She has arranged one last gift for her father on their trip. She has located James's birth mother's grave and even asked the cemetery attendants to clean it up. She drives her father there for what will be an emotional visit.

As he stands by the grave, he considers his life and the mother he never knew, the woman who gave birth to a four-pound boy and bestowed upon him maybe the only other thing she had to give: a name that recalled two men who mattered to her.

His mother is no longer here to share her story, but perhaps the extended family can tell him more when he meets them for lunch in Arkansas. In the meantime, there is just this patch of quiet ground and James's belief that the woman beneath it did her best.

His soft words are a reminder of how we might choose to live: "Human beings make mistakes. I have no anger toward her. I never have."

Perhaps that's a lesson he'll share with others as this reunion weekend develops. We have no way of changing the past. Anger and resentments can hold us captive there, bring us back again and again. Forgiveness frees us to move forward, into the now, into new possibilities, into the future.

———————

A small group of adoptees, including James, Millie, and Brigette, meander with Lisa and me into a special Kirby Pines dining room. Our conversation is already loosening up as we get to know one another, our voices louder and our laughter more frequent. White linen tablecloths cover tables that have been pushed together for our group, and a waiter brings us water and iced tea before we head for the serving line, where we share prolonged discussions on what dishes to choose, the same kind of chitchat I would have with old friends or at a family supper.

Among the folks I'm happy to get to know in person is Janie Brand. We've already chatted on the phone, and she's next up for an interview. She was one of the core group who helped pull this reunion together, and, sitting across from me at dinner, she perfectly combines good cheer and Southern graciousness. I'm also eager to look at the photos and paperwork she has brought.

Next to me sits my cousin Cindy, our photographer, and we're getting caught up on family news—our late mothers were sisters who died too young, and we've been close since. We segue to discussing tomorrow's schedule, and Cindy hops up to snap more photographs. I join in the chatter around the table and watch these budding friendships grow over shared chocolate chip cookies and bites of fruit cobbler.

I'm thankful. That's the best word I can come up with for this moment, and it fits.

CHAPTER 14

A PAIR OF BROWN
PAPER BAGS

———

"She left us on the courthouse steps."

SUE NELL IS ONLY THREE AND A HALF.

She doesn't understand what's happening when her mother deposits her, along with her five- and six-year-old brothers, outside the courthouse in Tiptonville, Tennessee.

They watch her leave. Then they huddle together on the steps and wait—for what they do not know.

A big black car arrives sometime later. A smiling older woman steps out and says, "Come with me." The children are ushered into the car by a chauffeur and a woman they believe to be a nurse.

The trip to the Tennessee Children's Home Society in Memphis is just over one hundred miles. The interstate has not been built. The winding state highway takes them farther and farther from their mama—and the sharecropper's shack that is home. At least they still have one another. They can survive that way. They've been doing it for a while now, brothers and sister hiding away together, dodging drunken tirades in their home and beatings delivered with the buckle end of a leather belt.

As the black car winds toward Memphis, the older woman promises them they are all going to the same place. They just need to be good little children. Cooperate. Behave. They sit silently in the comfortable seats. Brother Henry holds Sue Nell's tiny hand. Henry always protects her, if he can.

All will be well, so long as he's there.

But Memphis looms near now. The worst is about to happen.

Janie

JANIE BRAND, AGE SEVENTY-TWO WHEN WE MEET, MAY BE one of the last living adoptees who recalls Tann, the woman who affected so many lives. Unlike many who came and went as babies, Janie was old enough to observe Georgia Tann and to remember experiences in the big house on Poplar, Tann's notorious Memphis Receiving Home, which former staff members would later describe as a "house of horrors." The memories are imprinted on her brain and her heart.

Other adoptees attending the reunion are curious about that donated mansion, where their lives took sharp, unpredictable turns. They chat over muffins and scrambled eggs in our hotel's breakfast room and here and there in the hallways. A handful of them stayed up late last night in one of the rooms, talking over wine.

Despite the lack of name tags and an official opening event, strangers have become friends. Janie's story fills in gaps for the others. She's generous about sharing what she knows, and when we sit down for an interview in our hospitality suite at the hotel, she offers both painful and hopeful details. "The traumatic things, you remember," she tells me as we begin. "You can't erase a child's memory."

Her life before that day on the courthouse steps is also clear in her memory. Their mother, Eula, cannot read or write. Food is scarce—sometimes she has one egg to feed three children. They live in a sharecropper's shack in the country, with Horace. "This man who I knew as my father was beating the stew out of me," Janie says.

Her middle brother, Henry, practically a baby himself, frequently hides her in a cornfield to protect her. "Shhh," he whispers to her. "Don't let him find you." Sometimes he takes the beating himself, so she won't have to. The man, Horace, does not want the children. Doesn't like them. He's tired of providing for them, listening to their noise, putting up with them. Eula is pregnant again. These others are too much of a burden. He wants them gone, and so their mother loads them up and takes them to the courthouse.

Little Sue Nell has already experienced enough trauma for a lifetime—abuse, then abandonment. But now, as she is taken from the car at the Receiving Home on Poplar, she suffers separation from her brothers. "I know they took me from the car first on purpose and let the boys think they were coming, too," she explains. "My brother never would have let them get him out of the car without me."

That home is only for babies and toddlers. Older children are boarded at nearby orphanages and in unregulated private homes around the city. Tann knows how to separate siblings. She's good at severing the connections cleanly, abruptly, keeping the fuss to a minimum.

The loss will haunt Sue Nell for decades.

Sick with tonsillitis, she is swept into the frightening house on Poplar and kept upstairs in the nursery. The Tann environment isn't kind to sick children. According to orphanage records, she is treated with a glass of orange juice and a vitamin pill. "If I died, I died," she says.

Two weeks later, when her grandfather learns what has happened to the children, he drives to Memphis to get them back. An orphanage employee informs him that they have already been given away. "They are gone."

Sue Nell is just upstairs at the time.

Her brothers are at a different facility, a place that to this day remains unknown. All they will remember later is that there were nuns who wore habits. But they don't stay there long. Soon they are boarding a plane in the middle of the night with a Tann employee and several other adoptees. They're delivered to Hollywood, to satisfy orders in Tann's thriving market among celebrities and people with film industry connections.

The boys meet their new parents, Lana and Jonathan Snyder, in the lobby of the Fairmont Hotel, where the TCHS helper is quick to pass them off. The Snyders think they are twins and are charged one thousand dollars for each of them, nearly thirty thousand dollars today. The paperwork is handled by an attorney in a small West Tennessee town, who processed approximately two hundred TCHS adoptions through the Hardeman County Court, nearly all involving children sent to California or New York.

This rural county was reportedly chosen by Tann because California courts would not approve adoptions by unlicensed agencies. And TCHS was not licensed. In Memphis, a Shelby County judge would no longer okay Tann adoptions unless he interviewed the birth parents to make certain they were willingly surrendering their children; he also required the adoptive parents to appear in court for similar questioning. So the paperwork had been moved out into small towns. Tann had her ways of circumventing regulations of all types.

In California, Sue Nell's brothers don't settle in well. One scarcely speaks for a year. When the two do talk, they carry on constantly about a little sister. Finally, to quiet them, the parents adopt a baby girl for them. The adoptive parents pose all three for a round of photographs. The new family is complete.

SUE NELL, MEANWHILE, HAS been waiting alone in the house on Poplar Avenue. She has recovered from her illness, but the place is strange, frightening. "Every so often, they'd get a child, get them cleaned and dressed up, and then off they'd go," she remembers. "You'd never see them again." She also remembers a different mood in the house when Tann was there. The tension ramped up. Staff and children walked on eggshells, tried not to be noticed.

It is a skill Sue Nell already knew from her early years.

Learning to navigate life at the orphanage, she is unaware that plans are being made for her. She is destined for a Jewish home in New York. But that family, the one she was scheduled to belong to, is in Europe by the time Sue Nell is well and the call is made. *What would her life have been like if they had been home?*

At the orphanage, she continues to watch other children go through the ritual of being washed and dressed to attend parties to show them off or to meet their new parents. Then the day comes when the same thing happens to her. She knows what the hair bows and the pretty dress mean. "I was out in the swing when I met my parents. Mother and Daddy came out there, and I left and went home with them." The memory is so significant, she rephrases it as we talk: "I was in a swing in the backyard when my parents came, and I left with them that day."

She has to give the clothes back before she leaves. The brown paper bag of belongings she arrived at the orphanage with goes with her when she departs. Her new parents, Cecelia and Frank Hudson, take her shopping for clothes, and she is amazed to have new things of her own. She and her brothers never had anything new. They had hardly anything at all.

She is also given something else: a new name.

Sue Nell is gone.

She is Janie now.

Her adoptive mother is fifty-two years old and has been divorced once, and the couple's marriage is troubled—facts that, of course, the child does not know on this day. She's also unaware that a fee of one thousand dollars has changed hands. The cost of a pretty blond-haired girl. Her mother dresses her up and has a photographer take pictures, the girl's first portraits. As far as she knows, there were no photographs of her before that day.

This photo of Janie was taken on her adoption day. Movie stars, politicians, and other celebrities are part of Janie's childhood in Pulaski, Tennessee, and Key West, Florida.

A well-connected, politically active woman, Cecelia was born in New Orleans to a physician and his wife. She lived a glamorous life, including a stint as a Ziegfeld Follies showgirl.

Janie's adoptive father, Frank, is a Princeton graduate from a wealthy family. "I grew up with certain expectations and social attitudes," Janie says.

For a year after she leaves the orphanage, she lives with her parents in Pulaski, Tennessee. Her adoptive mother corresponds frequently with Tann, relaying what an adorable child Janie is and how much she loves her. Enclosed with letters are photographs, a standard practice for new moms eager to keep Tann happy. Those photos are used by Tann to market her services; she sends newsletters to prospective parents with information about the number of children TCHS "cared for" and the "happy homes" they found for those children.

When news breaks of Governor Browning's investigation into Tann in early September 1950, Cecelia immediately writes to the governor. His response is prompt and demonstrates her political connections. Ironically, it is dated the day after Georgia Tann died. "I did not act without knowing the facts in the case to a large extent," he says. "The matter was thrown at me, and the well-established proof that an individual was profiting personally from the operation of this Home seemed revolting to me . . . The flagrant betrayal of the trust in connection with the disposition of many babies could not go unheeded."

Browning cites the duplication of charges to adoptive parents and other benefits that went to the personal account of "an individual" instead of to TCHS. "Under no circumstances could I permit the continuation of a rank fraud," he writes. He also reassures Cecelia that the TCHS matter will not affect Janie's adoption. "She is a beautiful and adorable child. I see no reason why it should in any way touch her." He then promises Cecelia that he will do all in his power to see that foster parents waiting to finalize adoptions are not disturbed further "than to advise them of their misplaced confidence in one individual." He signs the letter, "With my warmest personal regards, I am sincerely your friend."

Janie's adoption is finalized, but as soon as that occurs, her parents separate. She and her mother move to Key West, Florida.

When she describes those next eight years, her face lights up. They are good ones. "I was an easy child. Not rebellious. Friendly." Cecelia is more like a grandmother to her and changes her life for the better, taking her away from *what if* to *what might be*, as Janie gratefully tells it.

For the first time, Janie's days are calm seas of certainty, predictability, reliability. Hope. Cecelia opens the world to her, another example of the difference one person can make. "She told me I could be anything I wanted." She exposes her daughter to famous people and elite functions, like a party for the Duke and Duchess of Windsor, who visit Key West on a Florida trip.

Cecelia is Janie's encourager, her stability.

Until she passes away when Janie is about to turn twelve. The girl is abandoned once more. The certainty is gone. The *what ifs* return. The preteen's whole life somersaults. Her adoptive father has remarried, and Janie must move back to his home in Tennessee. She has known Frank only from a distance, as a man who visited occasionally and brought a gift or two. His financial fortunes have turned since then. The home she's going to is humble. She must adjust to living in it with this virtual stranger and a stepmother.

Eleven months later, her adoptive father dies. "I had no real living relatives that I knew of," she says. With no place else to go, she stays with her stepmother, a far from ideal situation. "Those were tough years," Janie confides. "You always feel like you have a hole in your heart . . . You don't look like anyone else." Yet another impact on her life: "I would never date a boy who was adopted. I was afraid he might be my brother."

Now a mother of two children and a devoted grandmother, Janie has been divorced and remarried and is happy in her current phase of life, but she ponders whether her adoption affected her relationships through the years. "You always have the abandonment issues," she says with an attitude that is a mixture of realistic and sad.

For our meeting, Janie has brought along a story board full of photographs that detail her history. For her sake, I'd planned to keep our visit in the suite private, but other adoptees gather around us, eager to hear what Janie has to say, so we move chairs back and make room for them. Janie doesn't mind. With her reddish-blond hair, diminutive stature, and neighborly smile, she's a quiet woman of iron, made stronger, rather than having been destroyed, by the struggles in her early life.

Her take on her story is a positive one. Since the release of *Before We Were Yours*, she's been finding herself telling it more and more. She settles in to share the trail of events that have brought her to this moment. That's one thing all the participants here have in common. Each has a story of some random circumstance that ended up being the first step.

Janie finds out about the novel after seeing a brief mention of TCHS in another novel and writing to the author, Kathryn Cushman. Kathryn responds, saying she has always been interested in TCHS. She tells Janie about *Before We Were Yours*.

"I got the book from the library. I read about three chapters and said, 'I want this book,' and headed to the bookstore . . . This is my life. Everything in here . . . she captured it. I'm a hard critic because I lived it. I know how it was in real life . . . I started telling everyone about it. It's *my* story," she says again. "I wasn't a shantyboat kid, but I was a river rat."

A friend invites her to a discussion of the novel, her first experience with a book club. "I'd never attended a book club . . . it was very moving," she says. The club members think the historical novel is complete fiction, but Janie helps them understand that it is based on a true story. "This *really* happened," she stresses. "Let me tell you something . . ." she says to the group. And her story unfolds.

Speaking about her background helps others process their own experiences. "It's pulling things out of people and setting them free," she says. "Sometimes when you do something like this, it's sort of a pay-it-forward." Other book clubs hear about Janie and invite her to discussions about the novel, and over the coming months she speaks to more than a dozen groups. Then she sees that Lisa will be in Nashville in May and emails her, eager to share her story, so similar to the one in the book. She meets Lisa at a Nashville hotel; Janie pulls along her wheelie crate packed with scrapbooks full of adoption documents, printed emails from adoptee leader Denny Glad, yellowed TCHS brochures, cheery sales letters from Georgia Tann, adoption photos, birth-family photos.

The history of a life. And the history of many lives.

In the hotel, author and reader sit together, sift through the papers, talk about personal history, the histories of other adoptees, the upcoming reunion. Lisa is so caught up in the true-life story that so closely mirrors her novel that time zips by, and Janie warns that they'd better head for the bookstore hosting Lisa's talk that night. Though it's only ten miles away, Nashville's traffic is legendary.

Lisa never even moves her rental car from the hotel. She skates off with Janie, who drives like a ninja. After nearly an hour, they squeal into the bookstore parking lot with only five minutes to spare. Janie's daughter, Karen, comes from work nearby and meets them, eager to take in this part of her mother's history.

Other adoptees turn up in the audience as well: A woman whose adoptive parents were let into a hospital room with three babies in it and told they could pick one. A man who's spent his life trying to write the story of his adoption and his search but can't seem to distill it into the form he wants. He arrives with an armload of materials.

After the book event, Lisa, Janie, and Karen share a late-night dinner. They talk more about the history, about the connections of the next generation, why these stories should be told . . . but also about book clubs and parenthood.

Three weeks later, Janie is repeating her story again—at our reunion in Memphis, this time to me and to other adoptees and next-generation attendees who want to better connect with the legacy that is part of their family dynamics. She points to a photograph on her poster board. "This was made the day I was adopted," she says. We are captivated as she continues. I can see why she keeps getting requests from book clubs, inviting her to join in their discussions of the novel. "I'm coming wide open on this," Janie says. "It's so exciting."

It's then that I realize that this strong, upbeat woman has been a work in progress. Getting here has taken time—and has required her to overcome her fear of opening the Pandora's box of the past. She is sensitive to the fact that not everyone's desire to find a biological family will match hers. "Everybody doesn't have that need to know," she stresses to the other adoptees and family members gathered around us now. "If my adopted mother and father had lived, I would not have pushed."

She explains that after her adoptive parents' deaths, she felt unmoored, needed to reconnect with blood relatives and to search for the brothers she last saw in Tann's limousine. "I was always looking for someone to feel close to," she explains. Then she tells us about those brown paper bags—the one she carried as a three-year-old girl, and another one that would ultimately change her life, years later, reconnecting her with her birth family. "A little angel was on my shoulder that day," she says.

Telling this part of her story causes tears to rim her eyes.

In midlife, she signs up for a writing class taught by a retired teacher in Alabama. Students are instructed to bring something to write about, hidden in a brown paper sack.

Janie can't decide what object to take.

When it's time to walk out the door, she picks up one of Georgia Tann's Christmas books, a kind of catalog in which she pitched children to be adopted as holiday gifts. This is a subject about which Janie has something to say. But the writing teacher has a surprise in store for the class. Instead of writing about their own items, students are instructed to exchange the sacks. A male classmate receives Janie's—and has not a clue what it is or what to do with it.

He holds it up with a question.

The teacher is stunned. "Who brought this?" she asks abruptly.

Janie tentatively raises her hand.

"Where did you get it?"

"I'm adopted out of that home," she admits with trepidation.

The teacher, as it turns out, is also a Tann baby and one of the people who went to court with advocate Denny Glad to insist that Tennessee open its adoption records. She helps Janie connect with Denny and her volunteers. Although Janie had already obtained some of her records, Denny finds more. "The information she helped me get ended up answering questions I didn't know I even had," Janie says. "There was a lot of info there. I don't regret knowing. It's the story of my DNA, who I am."

Three weeks after they connect long-distance, Janie drives to Memphis to meet Denny. This hero of so many adoptees is ill and on oxygen, but it is clear to Janie that she is a powerhouse. They share a meal at a restaurant in a suburb and instantly bond. "I wanted to meet her and thank her in person," Janie says. "I learned a lesson long ago: *Never hesitate.* I think it comes from my adoptive mother dying so young. It was really nice to meet someone who worked so hard on our behalf. She saw a need and saw a way to fill it."

The pair continue their long-distance friendship and exchange lengthy emails for nearly seven years, full of the history of TCHS, Denny's efforts to locate birth families, and everyday details about things like the hassles of Christmas shopping and vacation travel plans. Janie keeps a file of all of their letters. "Her answers to me were wonderful. She had a tremendous impact on people. She was the push to get the identifying information."

Denny's commitment to helping adoptees resonates in the emails she and Janie share. "The need for truth can be so compelling," she writes. "I think it must be that need that overcomes all else." The official letterhead for Tennessee's Right to Know organization bears that one word: *TRUTH.*

And more truth is ahead for Janie. The answers to other longstanding questions come after another twist. At the time, Janie is doing temporary work, her assignments arranged by an employment agency. She is sent to Catholic Social Services, a charitable organization that helps people in need. The woman she works for arranges adoptions and listens to Janie's ongoing quest to find the brothers taken away all those years ago in Tann's big black limousine. "I've looked all my life," Janie says. Her boss tells her that the laws have changed, that Janie can contact the state of Tennessee and ask for additional information about her family.

She takes the steps required to learn more. Then the state of Tennessee writes to say they've found her mother. Janie hesitates, thinking it through. "The things I remembered about my mother, I was not sure I wanted to know this woman . . . I really wasn't looking for her, but I wanted to find my brothers." With misgivings, she places the call to her birth mother, Eula, who lives in rural West Tennessee. Maybe she will know where the two boys are.

The call doesn't initiate a happy mother-daughter relationship. "It was okay," Janie says quietly. "She was not who I was looking for." Her message to the woman who gave birth to her, then left her on the courthouse steps: "I maybe can get over it, but I'm not saying what you did was all right."

Even so, Janie and her husband drive to Tennessee to visit during the Christmas holidays, to see the world that would have been her life. A crowd has gathered on the front porch of Eula's house, and Janie can hardly force herself from the car. "I just sat there and looked at it and thought, 'I don't know if I can do this.' A lot of family members were sitting there that day. They didn't quite understand that I didn't want anything . . . I walked into this house with all this chaos." Most of the family had not known what happened to the three children way back when. "We just disappeared," Janie says.

Tsunami-sized culture shock roils over her as she sees Eula, and even today she sounds somewhat bewildered as she recalls the in-person encounter: "I never knew I was going to be meeting a group. You could tell that my mother wasn't sentimental. I asked her if she thought about us. She said, 'I figured there was no point, so I didn't.'"

Janie pauses.

Adoptees and family members in the conference room with us nod and wipe eyes. It's the response most adoptees fear when contemplating a birth-family reunion, the polar opposite of the dream: *I always loved you. I missed you. I thought about you every birthday all these years.*

All listen intently, their body language urging Janie to continue. But she steps away from her story to give a word of advice to the others in the room still looking for family members: "I strongly recommend one-on-one reunions."

Then she returns to her narrative about that brief holiday meeting with her birth family.

The day she sees Eula does yield a couple of special blessings. Amid the confusion, a farmer comes up on his tractor and asks her why she is there. When she tells him, he says, "I remember you. I remember when you were born. I knew your father." The visiting farmer was the owner of the sharecropper house where Janie lived. He owns it, still. She can come see it, if she likes.

Late in the visit, a red-haired aunt quietly pulls her aside. Janie has had the feeling several times that the woman wanted to tell her something—and it involves the man Janie has always believed was her biological father. "Horace wasn't your father," the aunt says. "I have a picture of your real father." Yet another shock.

For the first time, Janie learns that she does not carry the DNA of the man she remembers with such horror. Her birth father, a sharecropper, was shot on the banks of the Mississippi River in a gambling fight when Janie was just fourteen months old, too young to remember him. Her aunt gives her a grainy photograph of her father, the two little boys, and Eula, roundly pregnant with Janie. A family picture, posed by a photographer at a fair.

Janie can't help but wonder that day what she might have had in common with her birth dad. Later, she finds an old newspaper article and learns more about his death. In her birth mother, she sees mannerisms that are similar to her own. They've even decorated their houses with some of the same color schemes. Yet there is no emotional connection there, no joyful coming together. "I chose not to have a relationship with her," Janie explains. "She knew what she did, and I knew what she did."

Instead, Janie turns her focus on the search for her brothers. She learns that the boys were adopted by a general contractor and his wife in Hollywood and offered a good life, even getting to play on the MGM Studios lot. "They had it all," she says. "They had a swimming pool—these poor little boys who didn't have shoes before."

She finds out about their flight to California in the middle of the night, a common practice for Tann's operation. A babysitter took several children to the Fairmont lobby, to hand them over individually to their adoptive parents, people they had never met before. It was a favorite exchange point of Tann's. Continuing to search, Janie believes she has tracked down one brother, Henry, the one who protected her as a child. She attempts to contact the man she hopes will turn out to be him, and he calls back. His message on her answering machine thrills her: "I'm so glad to hear from you. I'm your brother." When they talk, joy enwraps her. "I remember *you*," Henry teases. "You were the little wet spot in the bed."

Janie's expression is tender when she speaks of finding her brothers, but the wound in her heart has not gone away. She reestablished a strong relationship with Henry, one they maintained until his death. "We got to spend twenty great years together," she says. "It was a wonderful twenty years." She points to a photograph on her display board. "This is us, after we got back together, sitting on those same courthouse steps."

Her other brother, Mack, who barely spoke during his first year after being abandoned, struggled with health issues as an adult and moved away from California. She has once more lost touch with him. She mourns the suffering all of them went though, as well as their separation. And she gives thanks for the answers to the mysteries that shadowed her for so long.

She tells of traveling to Nashville after finding her family, to thank the Tennessee Department of Human Services for helping her with her records. The two part-time employees in charge of adoption information are delighted. "We never get to meet the adoptees we helped," they tell her. Through DNA testing, more recently, she has connected with other cousins and is touched by these new relationships. Her comment echoes what I've heard so many TCHS adoptees say: "It was the first time I ever had seen anyone who looked like me." Janie goes on to say that for years she didn't feel the need to explore DNA results. "Then I did it and found two cousins . . . I said, 'Let's talk.' We're still in the beginning phase."

Her biological mother never expressed regret for what she did, even after Janie and her brothers reconnected with her. "She not only threw us away once. She'd thrown us away again," Janie says with anger.

But the bad memories mix with the good.

"I was not stolen," she declares. "Our mother just didn't want us. She was very, very poor. She left us on the courthouse steps, and I remember that . . . I'm sure it was a good thing I was adopted. I would've been twelve years old and pregnant if I had stayed." Her adoptive mother, in her life for only nine short years, saved her in so many ways and helped mold her into the woman she has become. "She always told me I was selected," Janie remembers. "She did everything she could to make me feel good about myself."

It is not the *what ifs* that fuel Janie now. She knows who she is. She tells her story to encourage others. She loves the children she gave birth to and raised, and the grandchildren who came next. She is also willing to keep exploring, to keep widening her circle of love.

Because who knows *what yet may be waiting*.

LATE ARRIVALS

When Robert walks into our Memphis hotel late in the evening, I am sitting with Lisa on a small sofa in the reception area. We are catching our breath after the day's emotional afternoon and equally emotional dinner at Kirby Pines.

A big man, Robert wears a stylish hat that is a cross between a fedora and a Stetson. His hair is gray underneath, and he exudes the confidence that has made him a successful insurance agent back in northwestern Arkansas. He's the kind of guy who probably can't walk a half block in his small town without greeting somebody he knows.

I make eye contact with him, the awkward glance of strangers looking for familiarity, wondering if they should know each other. *Are you here for the same reason I'm here?* the glance says.

Before he can move through the lobby, Lisa recognizes him and calls out. Only a little more than two weeks ago, she met him at a book festival in Arkansas and urged him to venture over to the reunion. When his daughter Heather had seen that Lisa would be speaking at the book festival, she'd encouraged her dad to read *Before We Were Yours*. With his history, she'd thought, it would interest him.

As he read the book, something shifted deep within him. "I think this really happened," he mused about the plot. Given his history, it felt real to him.

While the novel might have been the starting point for this unlikely trip, Heather is the true reason Robert is here, camping out in an unfamiliar hotel. She persuaded him to come, and he's here, steeling himself to jump into Saturday's activities.

Because it matters so much to Heather.

CHAPTER 15

SEVEN-DOLLAR BABY

---

*"My mother worried about them
coming and taking me away."*

Muriel and Chester Terrell are small-town folks in Washington County, Arkansas, salt-of-the-earth people. They always have food on the table, but the Great Depression has hit them hard. Money is tight. And yet, in 1936, they await a small miracle.

A *very* small miracle.

It is delivered to the back door of their house in a gleaming black car driven by a chauffeur. A woman in a nurse's uniform carries a bundle, the son they have longed for. Their baby, they are told, is just four weeks old. The name given to him at birth is Don Adley.

The adoption fee is seven dollars. Although that may not sound like much, it is a stretch for baby Don's new parents—about one hundred twenty-five dollars in today's terms. If the price had been any higher, they do not know what they would have done.

What's odd is that it isn't more. At the time, seven dollars is the official rate for an in-state Tennessee adoption. But the Terrells live *out* of state. And regardless of where the new parents live, healthy newborn boys command much more than the official rate from the Tennessee Children's Home Society. Extravagant fees for transportation and staff are eagerly forked over to Tann personally by yearning couples desperate to make their dreams come true. Favors are called in, and political and social connections utilized.

Checks providing generous donations to Georgia Tann's Memphis Receiving Home are written without hesitation, sometimes for years after the fact. Generally, Tann's customers are of the class that can easily afford it. Folks like Muriel and Chester don't typically get a baby delivered to their door three hundred miles from Memphis for that rate. *Did they know someone with a tie to the orphanage? Did a benefactor subsidize their payment? Or was Don born before greed completely swamped Tann's transactions?*

This bargain price will be a mystery, although not the only one, that will follow the innocent child, renamed Robert by his adoptive parents, throughout his life.

Robert

ROBERT TERRELL IS FULL OF RESERVATIONS AS HE AND HIS daughter drive to Memphis. His mixed emotions are making Heather feel as if she is forcing him to go—nonetheless, she is excited.

He insists on one thing: he will get back to northern Arkansas in time for the Razorbacks' playoff baseball game. He may let his daughter drag him to the informal Tennessee Children's Home Society adoptee reunion, but priorities are still priorities. He is *not* going to stay long in Memphis. After all, he's never cared about tracking down his birth family. His adoptive mother and father *were* his mom and dad. They were good people. They loved him and raised him up right. That's all he needs to know.

His daughter, however, wants to find out more. She's the one who first sent off for his birth records, twenty years ago.

A world of love rests in his decision to make the trip. He'd do anything for Heather.

Even this.

He is a "Georgia Tann baby," but his adoption and the history of his birth do not mean a darn thing to him. Or so he insists. "I didn't need to know. The only parents I've ever known were the parents who adopted me. I was adopted when I was four weeks old, to my knowledge. They gave me food, shelter, education, and love. I'm eighty-two years old and paid for. My mother said they delivered me to Springdale in a limousine."

Robert is comfortable in his own skin—and yet he is a contradiction of sorts. In spite of his sometimes blustery demeanor, he looks as though he could just as easily lean in and offer a bear hug. He is a hardworking man who still puts in full days at his insurance office, happy to offer customer service outside normal business hours. He does not want any surprises at this point in life. On the other hand, he loves his three children, and their questions propelled him to make this trip.

At age fifty-five, Heather is a striking woman, a mother, family caregiver, and book lover who has spent more than two decades looking for information about her father's birth family. Her smile is genuine. "He never wanted to find his birth parents, but he is open to it for us," she says, when we finally have time to talk.

LIKE MANY OTHER FAMILIES in the 1960s, Robert's adoptive parents maintain a combination root cellar and storm and bomb shelter. His mother keeps his adoption documents there in a faux-leather bank portfolio, instead of putting them in the safe-deposit box. Before her death, she anoints her granddaughter Heather to take charge of the records. "I want you to have them," she says. "You be the caretaker of these. You keep them safe."

So Heather does. She still has the portfolio, and she still keeps the papers in it. "My grandmother was uncomfortable with all of us finding out more about my father's adoption, but she knew the medical information was important."

The portfolio is with Heather on this trip. And on this night in Memphis, where his journey started, Robert looks at his adoption records for the first time—including letters from Tann, kept for all those years by his adoptive mother, and then by Heather. He studies the papers with her by his side in their reunion hotel suite. "All of those adoption papers, he had never even looked at," she says. The comment is startling and reminds me of how each adoptee approaches his or her mysteries differently.

As Robert examines the material, he becomes upset. "That kind of explains things; she was overly protective," he says of his adoptive mother.

Later Heather tells me the same thing about her grandmother. "She was just so protective of my dad."

ROBERT IS AN ONLY child who, with his parents, bounces among nine or ten houses in Springdale, Arkansas, during his childhood. He is much loved by the good-hearted couple. "They doted on me. I'm spoiled," he says with perhaps a hint of sheepishness as he and Heather tell me about his life.

Although he knows the name he was given at birth, the de-

Robert's adoptive mother, joyful in this photograph, worries that the Tann scandal will cause her son's adoption to be declared illegal.

tails of his birth date are confusing, even mysterious. "I'm not sure that birth certificate's right," he says. "We kind of suspect Georgia doctored that up or had it doctored."

His adoptive parents contacted TCHS months before they received him. A letter, signed by Tann, is written on February 6, 1936, addressed to the eager parents-to-be. "We regret our inability to fill all the applications we had for children during the Christmas holidays. We were deluged with letters and for this reason, we have been delayed in answering yours," Tann explains.

Then, in May 1936, Tann produces a child, writing about little Don: "We have a baby boy we believe you will be interested in, and the Worker has to make a visit to your home before a placement can be made. We ask that you send transportation to the amount of fourteen dollars, bus fare and incidentals. She will bring the baby to you and if you are entirely satisfied, we leave the baby. If not, the Worker will return him to the organization."

The letter is typed on TCHS letterhead with an old-fashioned silhouette illustration of a woman holding an infant in the air while two girls play nearby. But the content is not so heartwarming. Once more a child is treated as a commodity by Tann—a product, in this case, to be transported out of state.

At some point, the transaction for the boy shifts from bus to limo, though, and from fourteen dollars to seven. A home visit is not made. All part of the mystery. A hint that someone of influence might be pulling strings, though Robert and Heather have no idea who that could've been.

Robert is unsure how his parents connected with Tann. His mother, who had a miscarriage before the adoption, grew up in Helena, Arkansas, not quite seventy miles from Memphis. Since Memphis was the nearest big city for folks in Helena, it was not uncommon for them to travel across the state line for services. Could someone there have told his mother about TCHS?

His adoptive mother tells young Robert early on that he is adopted. Again, she is protecting him. She doesn't want him to hear it from someone else. Beyond that, the subject is not discussed. "I don't remember talking about it," he says. His father, a produce buyer, never speaks of it at all.

"I never felt 'less than,'" Robert insists. Yet when he proposes to his first wife, Heather's mother, he feels obliged to put his history on the table for consideration, explaining, "You might not want to marry me because I'm adopted." The unknown in their backgrounds looms large for Tann's former wards.

I've begun to notice an abundance of hints that point to the anxiety that has lingered for decades within families affected by Tann—both from mothers who gave up children and from mothers, like Robert's, who took them in and fell in love with them. Among all of the heart-wrenching records I've seen, one

Robert, adopted in small-town Arkansas and thankful to grow up there, avoids finding out about his birth family for years so as not to hurt his adoptive mother.

that affects me the most is a yellowed seventy-year-old newspaper clipping that Robert's mother saved, carefully folded up in her paperwork.

That brittle 1950 article reminds me of clippings I found after my own mother's death when I was in college. All sorts of articles had been stuck in her Bible or a cookbook or in the small metal file box that held our family papers. But Robert's adoptive mother's keepsakes convey her fear, all these years later, in underlined passages about the investigation into Tann and questions about the legality of Tann adoptions. The article proclaims in its headline that legislation may be needed to clarify the Memphis TCHS adoptions, and some may prove to be illegal. As I hold this article, Muriel's distress is palpable, even decades later.

Although she did not talk to Robert about the adoption, she certainly was *thinking* about it. Wondering about it. Agonizing over it. But until he sees the yellowed newspaper clipping while he and Heather are in Memphis, he does not realize the extent of her fear. "I'm sure she was scared they'd come and get me," he says, his perspective fine-tuned by the benefit of decades of hindsight.

Robert is fourteen at the time the scandal breaks, a happy teenager doing what teens do. His parents are terrified that their greatest fear—that this boy they've raised as their own could be taken away—is about to be realized. In desperation, they hire a lawyer they can scarcely afford to make certain the adoption is legal.

A series of typewritten letters from their Fayetteville, Arkansas, attorney gives a glimpse of yet more havoc wreaked by Tann. A letter dated November 1950 to the "Tennessee State Welfare Department" says, "I am taking this opportunity to write you in connection with all the trouble that you are having with the adoptions from the Tennessee Children's Home Society." The lawyer goes on to say that he represents Robert's parents. "Their main purpose in contacting us is to ascertain if the adoption of the above referred child was legal, and if it was not, what must they do."

The response would frighten any adoptive parent: "Should your adoption of your son prove in any way to be illegal, then you will be notified as to what steps must be taken . . ."

Robert's folks will not get the response they crave for six agonizing months. Finally, their attorney receives a letter from Lena Martin, by now state superintendent of TCHS in Nashville. "We believe," she writes, "from a review of our records, you may assure your clients there appears to be no reason for them to be concerned about the legality of this adoption."

Reading the letter, I imagine Muriel's trembling hands holding it, her eyes closing in gratitude.

"He had no idea that all of this was going on, that they had hired an attorney," Heather tells me, with Robert's files spread out on a hotel conference table in front of us. "Georgia Tann was always kind of a hero in his mythology; that was because she was a hero to his mother."

Some of those feelings remain. "I'm not mad at Georgia Tann," Robert says. "If she hadn't done what she did for me, I could be in jail. I'm not bragging, but I've done pretty well. I'm blessed. I'm eighty-two years old. It don't mean a damn."

Yet there have always been questions surrounding Robert's adoption. Information comes in odd ways, trickling in here and there over the decades. Heather reads a magazine article about Tann in the 1980s and becomes interested in finding more information. Once again, Muriel has the same reaction. "It really upset my mother," Robert admits. "She didn't like it." Nevertheless, her grandchildren are intent on learning more, particularly about their medical history. They search for information and accumulate quite a lot.

Heather's mother is interested for a different reason. She's into astrology and wants to know the time of day her husband was born. Perhaps this will help her understand his personality better—but his birth certificate is incomplete. She can't find the information she needs.

"We had to get a court order to get my birth certificate from the state of Tennessee," Robert tells me. The birth certificate reveals discrepancies. *Was he born on May 5 or August 31?* But Robert doesn't want to further upset his mother, so he backs off. "In some ways she felt threatened," he says, and the information was not important enough for him to push her. "It wasn't going to change anything . . . I didn't need to know."

When Heather's daughter is born, in 1990, Heather sees a news report about Tennessee's right-to-know legislation, which requires the state to provide records to adoptees. She works to find out more but does not tell her grandmother. She also turns to Denny Glad, who is mentioned in the news report. In several conversations, Heather finds Denny delightful and helpful, although Denny doubts that Robert was a stolen baby, because he was born in the mid-1930s, before Tann's criminal ways had escalated.

With the records open, any requests to the state of Tennessee must come from Robert himself. Still telling his children that he does not care about knowing, for their benefit he participates in this new search. In 1993, Heather and her siblings obtain the materials the state of Tennessee offers, information that does not reveal the identity of his birth family. "Then we just kind of stopped," she says. "We felt like our digging into it was making him sad. I was stepping on toes, and it wasn't worth it."

In 2005, when her grandmother Muriel dies, Heather says, "We kind of talked about it," but she and her sister-in-law, who has a PhD in history, cannot find information during this brief new search. The state says it looks as though both of the birth parents are deceased. Their names aren't in the current census.

Robert's second wife has him submit DNA through Ancestry .com and 23andMe. "I supposedly have a lot of cousins," he says. "I've never corresponded with them." He has not met any members of his birth family.

But after settling into the adoptee occasion in Memphis, sharing stories, and making a few new acquaintances, Robert is much more relaxed. He speaks with Heather about his adoption and his boyhood. He tells her about a woman who was shunned in his small Arkansas town because she had an illegitimate child. She could not come to town, and the little boy was not allowed to attend school. He tries to help Heather understand. In those days, the worst thing in the world was to be illegitimate.

His adoptive mother told him that he came from a large family and that they couldn't take care of him. *Was he born to an unmarried mother?* They do not know.

They may never know.

Then again, there are his children, whom Robert loves so, including Heather, who might have inherited a bit of her father's personality. Her tenacity never quite wanes. "There are so many points of interest," she tells me with conviction, "that keep bringing me back to look."

FAMILY "BIBLES"

———

That faux-leather bank portfolio, the keeping place of the disparate clues to Robert's biological history and mysterious adoption, is a potent symbol, I've come to realize. Everyone who shows up at our Saturday afternoon gathering for adoptees and families has their own version of it. Lillian has her tote bag full of records. Connie has her binder. Janie has her wheelie crate. Brigette carries a notebook straining against the reams of information about the family members she has finally uncovered for her father, James.

A manila folder here. A display board there. An old shoebox.

A plastic tote with a snap-on lid.

The attendees place these items with care on the library's stately antique wooden tables. Our reunion group is meeting in the Benjamin L. Hooks Central Library, in the Memphis and Shelby County Room on the third floor, the space that houses the official archival collection of materials about Georgia Tann and the eventual demise of her empire.

But these adoptee "bibles" are a smaller, more personal type of archive. They're filled with decades-old records and details of what has often been an excruciating search, bits and pieces of a poignant heritage in plastic sleeves: black-and-white photos of adoption day; the only picture of birth parents; a newspaper clipping about Tann's misdeeds; records from TCHS, retrieved from the state of Tennessee

at a cost; original birth certificates; court filings; sometimes letters to
and from Tann herself.

*Scraps of paper
here, letters there,
tell of the anguish
that adoptive
parents go through
as they deal with
Georgia Tann.
This article raises
fear in Robert's
mother's heart that
he will be taken
away from her.*

Some adoptees have added brief typewritten histories, maybe a
page or two, showing time lines and milestones. Others have charted
each step they've taken to make the Rubik's Cube of their lives come
together. During the reunion, attendees spread out the contents and
explain how they found this or came across that. They are eager to
help one another locate whatever is available and to learn of new resources.

These adoptee "bibles" are a unique kind of family treasure, and
their contents have been hard won.

———

As adoptees and their families wander among the library tables and
display boards, a hum of emotion rolls through the room. The Random House film crew is interviewing Connie and Lisa over by a wall
of windows. Cousin Cindy is scurrying around the room capturing

each person with her camera, then turning to photograph documents that I will use later in researching their stories. James stands before a photo of Tann on an easel and playfully pretends to poke it with his cane. Janie offers insights to four sisters who have come here in an effort to understand their adoptee mother's story better.

This room, as my Grandma Brosette would have said, is working alive, and it takes me a moment to identify what I'm seeing. It's *empathy*. These reunion attendees understand one another's journeys like no one else can, and they feel for one other. It's like being in a foreign country and running into a dear friend from your high school.

I notice a newcomer clutching his file, and I head his way. I know that whatever his story is, it will be something I want to hear.

CHAPTER 16

THE COURT CASE

"They were good to her . . . but they
also wanted someone to help around the house."

———

CROPS FAIL ON THE FORTY-ACRE FARM IN NORTH GEORGIA
in the summer of 1923. Roscoe Tuggle, a desperate father, has
to earn more money, so he leaves home in search of work and
finds a job in a steel mill in Beach Bottom, West Virginia, firing
a stationary boiler engine for sixty-seven cents an hour.

His wife, Ella, and their three young children stay behind,
anxiously awaiting word from him, with enough corn for them
and the livestock for a limited amount of time. Roscoe sends
money for a while, but then his correspondence grows scarce.
Finally Ella receives a $100 money order from her husband.
She sells the mules, cows, and chickens and packs up the children, spending the money to travel to Maryville, on the far east
side of Tennessee, where she has a relative.

In the small town, she struggles to support her family. She
has run out of money, and with no resources and no sign of
Roscoe, she leaves the kids in the care of the Blount County
Industrial Home, planning to find news of their father and
come back for them. She takes a job as a cook in a nearby camp
and pays their board. The paperwork she has to sign, though,

in order to keep them there, has a devastating word at the top, one she does not adequately understand. *Surrender.*

She thinks she's leaving the kids temporarily.

The Tennessee Children's Home Society decides otherwise. Within weeks, on November 22, 1923, an unsigned letter from the TCHS superintendent's secretary is sent to the Industrial Home, asking for more information about one of the children. "The child is a good risk," the Blount County home official writes on the paperwork. A postscript typed at the bottom reads:

> The children are beginning to get acquainted with us and the teacher in the school has complimented them very much; they are, we think, very sweet children, and all very pretty.

Roscoe eventually has the money to send for his family, and he finds Ella; but when they try to reclaim their children, they learn that they have been taken. Confused and with money tight and communications difficult, they are not sure what to do. He and Ella, their relationship reportedly rocky, settle in West Virginia without the three kids, establish a new home of sorts, and have two more children. Nevertheless, they are determined to find their other kids.

Roscoe and Ella manage to save up—not easy to do—and eventually strike out for the TCHS Nashville office, but the employees there will not tell them where the children are. Desperate, they use every penny they have to hire a well-respected Nashville attorney, paying him five hundred dollars—about seventy-five hundred dollars now—a huge sum for them. Mentioned in the court papers is the surprise of the officials at the steel mill where Roscoe works that he'd go as far as spending that kind of money on an attorney to get his children back.

An extraordinary legal battle gets under way, a rare attempt to take on TCHS and Tann very early in her career.

The stricken couple spends four years—and money they can ill afford—trying to find their kids. They are poor Southerners and not well educated, the kind of people who cannot ordinarily wage such a battle. But they want their children. Amazingly, against the greatest of odds, they succeed in locating two of the three, something Tann went to great lengths to prevent from happening. Only they are told that they cannot have those two children back. Their third child is never found.

William

WILLIAM TIMMONS EASES INTO THE LIBRARY ON THE SATURDAY afternoon of the reunion. He joins the group at the oak tables, bringing information of his own and a story about a pursuit of justice. His mother was one of the three siblings taken from what their mother intended to be a temporary stay in the Blount County Industrial Home and placed in adoptions by TCHS. The papers William carries are devastating—in particular, the documents from the lawsuit his biological grandparents filed while fighting to recover their children.

Now age seventy-two and the father of two grown daughters, William says he hopes the story of Tann's misdeeds will be publicized as much as possible. "I'm not sure people are aware this went on for thirty years," he tells me as we move to one of the library tables out of the way. With a trim beard, wire-framed glasses, and blue jeans, he looks like the custom-furniture builder and contractor he is, as he shares his family's tragic story in quiet but urgent tones. He has been shaken by what happened, and it has affected his life in myriad ways. He is a paradox: he wants people to know and yet is resigned to the past.

He offers to let me review his personal collection of evidence, then mail it back. I am afraid to take the originals of something so precious. I scrounge in my purse for change to make copies, fumble with the library copier, and do the best I can, William looking over my shoulder.

"A lot of people still feel this way, that people who are poor deserve to be . . . but they're just people," William says, visibly angry about this injustice visited upon his family—and others like them—two generations ago. "Evil stuff."

The documents and William tell the story of a little girl caught in the crossfire of poverty, greed, and a system that favored money over biology.

MAUDE IS SEVEN YEARS OLD when her mother drops her off at the home, thinking it'll be for only a little while. Maude is at a cute age, but she's already too old to be a favorite for adoption. "Most people, they want a baby," William remarks as we leaf through the records together.

So Maude is placed with a foster family in Memphis, and her name is changed to Margie. Her younger brother, Larry, age five, is sent to a different Memphis household and named Caleb. For about four years, Ella and Roscoe search and search and, in what seems like a miracle, Roscoe finds both of them. He cannot find the youngest, Estelle, age three.

As Ella and Roscoe expend every resource they have to get their children back, the tragic drama plays out in the courts in Tennessee. Legal papers and newspaper stories paint a wrenching picture, the struggle of a poor family pitted against an all-powerful machine. The articles and testimony smear their names, the details spelled out in letters to court officials and a lengthy, sloppily typed "Story Sheet" dated May 16, 1927, and compiled by TCHS for its orphanage files.

The Story Sheet plays up Roscoe and Ella's marital problems, the hostile involvement of Roscoe's mill employers, and the poor condition of their house in West Virginia.

> The house is composed of two rooms, window in each end—over the window was brown paper. No out house except a half built and half finished garage, a broken down Ford car with three wheels and a badly torn top was the car referred to in [Mr. Tuggle's] statement that he would take the children to and from school in.

While Roscoe maintains that his wife was forced to sign the papers surrendering the children, his boss and others at the mill, who are increasingly involved in the case, call that claim ridiculous. Documents recount the boss saying that if Roscoe will give up bothering the children in their present homes and take care of the two children born "since the other children were deserted," he and the other men at the mill will stand by Roscoe. If, however, the father persists in disturbing the children, he will never receive assistance. The paperwork builds, taking in a roster of people who either do not know the Tuggles well or are on the mill's payroll but still are asked to give depositions. A justice of the peace writes a letter saying that the depositions will have to be scheduled around his full-time work . . . at the steel mill.

Despite the obstacles, Roscoe, thirty-three, reunites with his children, a heartbreaking event captured in the *Memphis Evening Appeal* newspaper right after it occurred.

Coverage in the Memphis Evening Appeal
describes the battle for the Tuggle children.

"Brother, do you remember me?" Maude, now eleven and called Margie, asks while hugging her brother, now called Caleb and nine years old.

The bewildered boy shakes his head.

Roscoe, a muscular steelworker, picks up the child. "Sonny, do you remember me? I'm your father, boy."

The boy again shakes his head, frightened. Then he cries. Roscoe puts his son down and says, "I . . . I guess I have sought them these four years for nothing. He don't remember me, and the courts won't give them to me."

The court, however, has not ruled yet, so Roscoe fights on. Both Maude's foster mother and Larry's new parents say they will give the children back to Roscoe if the court rules they must. But Roscoe has already picked up on hints. Too much power rests on the other side of the argument, too much money and influence. Their children are never coming home.

The court provides justification in its comments. The judge describes Ella as a misguided mother who gave her children away and who associated with improper people, although Roscoe maintains again that she did not know the ramifications of the paper she was forced to sign at the Industrial Home. When the ruling is handed down, it contains pages of typewritten, old-fashioned legalese. The judge laments having to rule in a domestic matter and cites Roscoe's rights as a husband and father. Then he decrees that the two children cannot go home with their birth parents and will stay where they are.

The court agrees with Tann and the Tennessee Children's Home Society—that children are better off in homes where they can have nicer clothes, better surroundings, and parents with means. "Could they not be shaped into children who fit in the new environments where they landed?" the judge writes. "Should I, under these circumstances, take these children from homes of culture and refinement, where I am satisfied they are cared for and given proper educational training?"

But Roscoe and Ella simply cannot give up. They continue the fight, hoping to use their suit as a test case. Although the judge takes the case under advisement, by now the family's resources are depleted. With next to no money, growing worries about confusing little Maude and Larry further, and the inability to even locate their third child, they finally concede the inevitable. The couple's attorney delivers a simple and chilling message to the court: "Mr. Tuggle has decided not to fight the case further."

That single, brief, complicated encounter with their birth family during the original court case is the last one little Maude and Larry will ever have.

Larry/Caleb remains in a home with a family that has one biological child. That presents complications further along, an issue that finds space in Tann's paperwork some years later, when she weighs in on young Caleb's situation in a letter to Fannie B. Elrod, then state superintendent of TCHS in Nashville. In the letter, Tann remarks that something has *bobbed up* with the Tuggle son. The man who took him wants to change the boy's last name but not officially adopt him—to keep him from eventually sharing property and financial inheritances with the family's natural child.

"It is hard for me to conceive of people who have had two children all of their lives and do not care enough about them to want them to share in their finances as well as in other ways," Tann complains. "It makes you feel like telling him that we did not ask him to take the children or to spend anything on them."

Maude/Margie lives with her long-term foster parents, described as a prominent family, until she marries. "They were good to her and loved her," William tells me, "but they also

wanted someone to help around the house . . . They were probably better than some of the adoptive parents." By the time
William is in his twenties, he knows there is something strange
about the family's situation. His mother's brothers are a good
deal older than she is, and everyone refers to them as his "uncles," but he knows he isn't related to them. "No one talked
about it very much," he says.

Then a cousin mails him a packet of family material, including the lawsuit. His family's hidden history leaps from the
pages. Over the years, he has contemplated the matter a great
deal but has not searched for other relatives. About ten years
ago, he and his cousin heard a story about how the Tuggles'
lost younger daughter, Estelle, was adopted in California by a
car dealer after Tann took her from the Industrial Home.
"Whether that's true or not, I don't know," he says. He does
not see much point in requesting records from the state of
Tennessee.

Sitting with me at our quiet library table, William shakes
his head. "I'm okay now, but the whole thing has been kind of
painful to me," he says. The political and financial game that
was played in Memphis hit his family square in the heart. His
deep feelings go beyond his own family, however. He wants the
horror to be publicized for other families and is still shocked by
the idea that so many people were willing to ignore such a cor-
rupt system.

"I assume my real grandparents were unusual in finding my
mother," he says. "It is hard to believe that sort of thing went
on." William's submerged outrage is almost palpable, but he
hopes that something good came out of the family's pain. Perhaps his grandparents gave courage to other families, inspiring
them to look for their children and to challenge TCHS.

Maybe by talking about this now, he's doing his part to take up arms in the battle his grandparents Roscoe and Ella fought to the last of their resources. And maybe a grandson's efforts to share their story can help prevent this sort of tragic situation from ever happening again.

NEWLY
EXTRAORDINARY

———

*S*trangers regularly come up to me in the town where I grew up and exclaim, "You must be related to . . ." They proceed to name one of my three brothers or a nephew. A former newspaper colleague ran into my middle brother at church recently and immediately pegged him as one of my kinfolks. I've been asked so many times if my nephew is my son, I've quit counting.

We are genetically stamped, and that resemblance, complete with my father's nose, is something I've never thought too much about.

Lisa, too, favors her brothers. When they are together, they speak alike, walk alike, gesture the same ways.

After this weekend, we will never again take those blessings for granted. Lisa and I have been given the chance to imagine what it's like to spend your life wondering who you look like, searching faces in crowds thinking, "Does anybody here look like me?" Never to attend a big holiday meal surrounded by people who share your hair, eyes, build, mannerisms. Never to have an aging aunt say, "You look just like your father."

These everyday things don't always seem that valuable. They even go unnoticed in the moment. Until you come face-to-face with someone who doesn't have the luxury of such a connection. Then the ordinary takes on new meaning. It becomes a gift to be appreciated and treasured.

Never again to be seen in quite the same way.

———

When I said yes to Lisa's invitation to capture these real-life stories, I did not expect to learn a lesson at every turn, but I should have known better. Each of these families has been changed by the way they encountered Georgia Tann. Each brings a lesson.

And another lesson lies just ahead.

CHAPTER 17

THE NIGHT ALL
THE BABIES DIED

―――――

"I didn't understand the agony
they were going through."

THE YOUNG MOTHER-TO-BE GOES INTO LABOR IN THE MIDDLE
of the day. Her husband is at work, and a telephone is not available. He cannot be reached until the end of his shift. A neighbor
takes Josie Henderson, not quite twenty-one, to the maternity
ward at the hospital in Memphis. Another neighbor stays with
their toddler daughter.

Excited about her new child, Josie gives birth to a baby boy
late that afternoon. The eager father, Noah, arrives at the hospital that evening, after work. He admires the new arrival
through the nursery window. The baby is crying, strong and
healthy. Their first son.

Josie is still in the maternity ward the next morning, foggy
from the lingering effects of the anesthetics, when the hospital
officials deliver devastating news.

Their newborn son has died overnight.

She overhears the other mothers also being told that their
babies died during the night. She's confused, disoriented. Grieving. In shock. Unsure of herself in the moment. She and her
husband do not have money for a funeral. They have no idea

how to handle the logistics of the tragedy. The paperwork and the details are confusing for two young parents, each only able to obtain an eighth-grade education before going to work.

Unimaginable grief rushes in. Life turns upside down.

Workers at the hospital tell the new mother that the hospital will handle everything and take care of the body. All she has to do is sign.

Stanley

WHEN HE ENTERS THE HOOKS LIBRARY FOR THE AFTERNOON gathering of adoptees, it is clear that he is not sure he should have come. And yet it seems he could not be anywhere else.

Perhaps only a deathbed promise to his mother could have gotten him here. Or maybe his deep love for the brother he never met. With his hair and mustache both gray and his car keys on a lanyard around his neck, he looks tentative yet determined in this wood-paneled room filled with information about Tann and TCHS. Now retired and living in Arkansas, Stanley Henderson is seventy-two when he drives to one of the book events on Lisa's All Arkansas speaking tour. Today he drove nearly the same route his parents took when his brother was born and then, shortly afterward, he thinks, was stolen from the hospital maternity ward.

He wants to believe that his brother, who would be seventy-eight now, is still alive. Out there somewhere. For years he has carried his brother's name and birth date, DAVID CLINTON HENDERSON, AUGUST 31, 1939, on a piece of paper in his wallet. "I wanted to make sure I never forgot it," he tells me as we find a place together at a quiet table. I turn to a fresh page in my spiral notebook and begin taking notes.

Stanley has no idea what his brother's adopted name might be, nor where he might have been taken as a baby, or where he might be living now. The baby who was born David Clinton could be living two blocks from this library or two thousand miles away. Stanley has no way of knowing, and so he's come here to this gathering, to see if there's a way to find out. Anything he hasn't tried yet. "I'm going to tell you the truth," he says. "I have just about given up hope. I have run into so many dead ends."

BABY DAVID IS BORN in John Gaston Hospital, itself a character in this family's heartbreaking story. An impressive building financed in part by the Works Progress Administration during the Great Depression, the hospital was the birthplace of many babies appropriated into Tann's system.

The building is demolished in 1990 to make room for a modern regional health center. Ironically, it is wiped off the face of Memphis about the time that Denny Glad and her volunteer corps finally succeed in forcing the state to open its adoption records and a large number of TCHS babies renew their searches for their history and medical records.

But for David's grieving family, there are no records to be found. It is as if their son never existed at all. And yet the more his mother's memory clears and the family's grief subsides, the more things don't make sense. How could multiple mothers in the same ward receive the same news? How could *all* the babies born in the hospital that night—with at least three mothers in the delivery ward on the day Josie remembers, and maybe more—have died so quickly?

The questions haunt the family.

Through the days that follow, they put clues together and

conclude that their son has been stolen—along with other babies in the nursery that night. They never believe that the baby died. Only they don't know what to do about it. They have never heard of Georgia Tann and the Tennessee Children's Home Society. They are unaware of Tann's frequent appropriation of newborns by the easiest, cruelest possible method: simply telling birth mothers that their babies were stillborn or died shortly after delivery.

Even though Josie and Noah know nothing about the powers at work in and around Memphis, they believe to their core that someone took their baby boy. They are certain of it.

But life moves on, and they must, too.

The day after baby David's birth and disappearance, Adolf Hitler mobilizes his plan to invade Poland. The start of World War II causes U.S. factories to be retooled for war efforts. Women enter the workforce in large numbers. The couple moves from rural Arkansas to Los Angeles to work for Lockheed Aircraft. Josie installs running lights on the wings of B-17s. Noah works on the assembly line.

Near the end of the war, production slows, and the Hendersons move to West Memphis, Arkansas, to be near relatives. Upon their return to the area, they hear about Tann.

To them, the news confirms what they have long believed, that their son was stolen. They do not talk about it, though. For years, they hold this bitter secret inside themselves. It affects their lives in varied ways. They have other children, but they never get over the loss of their first son. "They just couldn't bring themselves to tell me about it," Stanley says. He's emotional as we sit at the library table together. It's hard for him to talk about this family tragedy, which predates his birth by several years. "I wish I could have helped."

When Josie becomes pregnant with Stanley, their next child

after David, the lost baby, she refuses to go to the hospital. Terrified of what could happen, in September 1945, she gives birth at home, where it's safe. Growing up, Stanley always knows that there is something unusual about his birth. Not until decades later does he learn why his mother insisted that he be born at home.

"I knew my mother had had a baby . . . I didn't know much else. I grew up not knowing about this because she didn't talk about it. One time I tried to ask her," he recalls. "They didn't want to talk about it," he says again, his voice mournful.

That conversation—or the lack of it—hurt him as well as his parents. What goes unspoken between them that day continues to hover around the edges of various conversations for years. Every once in a while, it elbows in. When Stanley's own son is born in the late 1960s, family members sit in a hospital waiting room, excited and anxious about the birth. "I hope everything goes well," one person says.

"This always goes well," another replies.

Noah, Stanley's father, speaks, his voice somber: "You don't know. Strange things can happen."

Stanley is puzzled by the remark, by the sense of foreboding it brings into the room. "The strange way he worded it . . . it has stuck with me my whole life."

In later years, Josie is diagnosed with breast cancer. When she becomes seriously ill, small details about her firstborn son trickle out. "The more I learned, the more I felt guilty," Stanley says. Yet he was afraid to reopen old wounds. Now he wishes he had. "I didn't understand the agony they were going through. Just imagine. She's twenty years old, and this authority figure in the hospital tells her to sign papers."

In the 1990s, Stanley's family, like so many others, sees a television news piece on efforts to open Tennessee's adoption records. "I contacted these ladies," he says. "They were swamped after *60 Minutes*." He continues his search on his own, and then, just three days before his mother's death, she tells him that his big brother was not named at the hospital but after they came home.

Stanley is stricken to realize that all this time he has been using the wrong name in his search. He knows his brother as David, but that almost certainly would not have been his name when he was given to a new family.

As Stanley's mother prepares to die, she talks more. "She wanted David to know he was not given up. He was wanted and loved," Stanley says. He promises his mother on her deathbed that he will never stop looking for David. "For the first time in my life, she talked the way I wish she had." He doesn't blame his mother, though. As a young man, he admits ruefully, he was more interested in things like his 1956 Chevrolet.

In the news, Stanley hears about a serial killer identified by DNA on the West Coast. His hopes are renewed. DNA provides a new avenue that could lead him to his brother. His sister submits her DNA to a national database, and he studies her results, which include relatives they know, and this gives Stanley confidence in the test's accuracy. It also names cousins known and unknown. The test does not, however, give them their brother. Another hope ends in a dead end.

For a few years, he gives up. "I dropped the ball on that promise I made to my mother," he admits. "It was just too hard." In 2017, though, he comes across the novel *Before We Were Yours*, and the topic catches his attention. He downloads the book and reads about the river rat family whose children are stolen from their shantyboat at Mud Island. "It magnified for me the agony my parents must have been going through," he says. He recalls driving by Mud Island on the Mississippi

River in Memphis when he was a young man. "I remember us making fun of shantyboats then. I wouldn't do that now."

The telling of the story in the novel stirs within him some measure of optimism. He visits Lisa's website and sees that she will be in a small town less than an hour from his home as part of her All Arkansas tour. He gets into his car and drives over before he can talk himself out of it.

This is Lisa's last stop before Memphis, and Stanley approaches her with earnest words. "Could you sign the book in memory of David Clinton," he asks. As she signs the novel, he forces out the words: "That's my brother who was stolen by Georgia Tann." His eyes film with a haze of tears. He cannot hide his emotion when she looks up, but then again, there's no reason to. She knows the devastation left in Tann's wake. She urges him to come to the adoptee reunion, happening in just a few days.

He is reluctant. "I've heard about it," he says. "I emailed a lady . . . but that's just for TCHS adoptees and their families."

"It's for anyone connected to the TCHS adoptions," Lisa reassures him. "To tell the stories, but also to share resources and ideas that could help."

After leaving the book event, Stanley is at war with himself. Should he go? Talking about his brother is not something he has done through the years. He has never even fully told the story to his children, and he has not told anyone else except his pastor at the church he attends. Nonetheless, courage propels him. He is a quiet man of honor and faith, and his promise weighs on him.

When participants at the TCHS reunion are invited to the front to speak, Stanley is overcome with emotion and declines to join them. But the stories of the others grip him. They are adoptees who've followed trails to find answers about their pasts. He is still wondering if there is any trail to follow. And yet he must try. He is especially moved to hear the story from a man who never knew why his mother gave him up. *Was that man's mother coerced into signing papers while she was still under anesthetic? Could she, like Stanley's parents, have mourned and agonized over unanswered questions for years?*

He chokes up again later as he discusses this with me during a phone call. On his drive home from the Saturday afternoon gathering, he admits, he kicked himself for not having spoken up at the library, for not telling his family's story. "I wish I would've kept my emotions under check."

But in some moments, the loss and the pain are too deep for words.

And that promise he made to his mother on her deathbed— that he wouldn't stop looking? He won't. The stories of others have given him at least a small measure of hope.

Maybe his brother is out there. "Maybe someone will find him," he says.

Maybe someday he'll have a reunion of his own.

WHAT IF?

———

The story Stanley told, about searching for his brother stolen at birth, hits me hard, in part because he is so like my older brothers: lean, plainspoken, and down to earth. I can imagine the two of them coming into the Memphis library, hesitant but committed. We are rural Arkansas natives, similar in many ways to the people I meet through this reunion. How would my family's life have been different if one of my beloved brothers had disappeared at birth? The idea shakes me.

Stanley tells me that one of his main reasons for talking with Lisa and me is to encourage families to do a DNA test. "If you know of anyone, please use the DNA test," he says. "The way I look at it, this DNA is my only hope. My biggest request for anyone ever adopted through the Tennessee Children's Home Society would be: Do the DNA test."

It's not a new message in these stories, and I myself have seen its vital role in the hands of teenage Josh, James and Brigette, and genealogist Linda, who helped James track down his birth relatives. This devoted genealogy sleuth has made a life's mission of tracing families, volunteering hours each week to extract information from records and enter it into a computer. The interest in family history has increased dramatically, thanks in large part to new technology. "All over the world, they just have that desire to know their roots," she says.

The words raise questions for me, make me wonder if my family might have secrets. My husband is a West Tennessee native. Could he have relatives caught up in the TCHS scandal?

He and I order DNA kits and submit them, which feels way more personal than I expected. No surprises pop up on my side, but my husband finds a few relatives he has never heard of, including an unknown first cousin in Memphis.

We begin our own search, wondering what mysteries might be hiding behind the name.

————

A group of sisters, the daughters of a child stolen from her front yard and put up for adoption by TCHS, have joined us for the weekend and added an entirely different perspective to the reunion. They are my last planned interviews, and I wonder briefly how I will keep pace with all four of them when we sit down together. But they have been engaged, enlightening participants this weekend, so I suspect they'll show me mercy if I have to ask them to slow down.

CHAPTER 18

FOUR SISTERS

———

"I'm the child of a stolen baby."

NELDA SUE IS PLAYING IN THE YARD OF THE FAMILY'S riverbank shack with her twin sister, her younger brother, and two younger sisters when Georgia Tann's big, beautiful black car drives up. The window rolls down.

Do the kids want to go for a ride?

Of course they do.

Children of searing poverty, they climb in, dazzled by such luxury. Nelda and her twin are six, although their ages will be in dispute for the rest of their lives. The middle sister is four or five. Their brother is three. The baby girl is not even a toddler.

Their mother has been beaten up during a domestic dispute and has landed in the hospital. Worried that they don't have anyone to look out for them, she signs papers that she believes will put the children safely into foster care until she's well. She's unaware that the kindly people who have promised to help her have instead put her on the target list. Nelda Sue's mother has already lost her children; she just doesn't know it yet. Days later, when she asks for them, she's told she cannot have them back, that they have already been given new homes.

Desperate, she finds her way to the orphanage and stands

outside the fence for days. Finally, she sees one of her daughters. The child asks to go home with her. But the fence is too high, and the orphanage personnel will not open the gate.

There's nothing she can do. Her children are already destined for other places.

Vivian, Paula, Elinor, and Kate

NELDA'S DAUGHTERS KNOW—HAVE ALWAYS KNOWN—THAT AS a child their mother was stolen from a shanty on the banks of the Mississippi River.

Her story, and its effect on their lives, is what has brought them here today.

Accomplished and thoughtful women, they gather with Lisa and me in our hospitality suite—the hotel meeting room with its round folding tables and sturdy chairs, grocery store flowers, and lukewarm bottled water.

I settle in at a table in the corner with these four lovely women who are all about my age. I, who have no sisters, try to imagine what it must be like to be one of four. That they are all here together is improbable. That they came as a group to open themselves to the experiences of this weekend feels almost inevitable. A long and, at times, excruciating history propels Vivian Morrison, Paula Kennedy, Elinor Harris, and Kate Price to our equally improbable reunion.

They've come for many reasons. Understanding, the sharing of a story, another step in a hard-won battle to discover new compassion for their mother, and kindness for themselves.

They also seek peace for her, the final resolution of a life that was never quite settled. Her ashes accompany them to Tennessee. "I had always made a promise to my mother that I would bring her back, so she was coming with us," says Kate, who, at fifty-nine, is the youngest sister.

They begin by telling me the story of what happened to young Nelda Sue.

AFTER A SHORT STAY at TCHS in Memphis, Nelda and her twin are put on a train to Philadelphia with a TCHS employee. The girls are told their siblings will arrive on the next train and meet them there.

But they never come.

A cheerful woman, a schoolteacher named Doris Harris, greets the two little girls. "I'm your new mommy," she says.

"Oh, no you're not," Nelda replies. "You're not my mommy."

Nelda Sue's name is tweaked to Nelda Suzanne. Her last name changes, too, of course. As reluctantly as she takes on the new name, she takes on her new adoptive home and parents. A lifetime of fighting, resentment, and uncertainty follows. Although her twin seems to accept their changed circumstances, perhaps with some degree of resignation, Nelda refuses.

Nelda is taken from her river shanty home and relocated by train to Philadelphia.

She is old enough to remember her life before adoption—how Tann's car took her away, how she helped with diapers and running and fetching at the orphanage before she was adopted. How she had a brother and sisters. And a mother.

The family is separated for decades, and Nelda's life is full of confusion, anger, and rebellion, as well as a sense of shame that she will pass along, in a variety of ways, to her children.

She is always to wonder what life would have been like if they had not been stolen.

As a teenager, Nelda follows the path of many troubled youths and starts her own family early. She becomes pregnant with Vivian when she is only fifteen and marries the sixteen-year-old father. By the time she's in her early twenties, she has four daughters and a son . . . and no ability to mother them. She and her husband fight constantly and are soon divorced. The siblings' father disappears from their lives, not to resurface until they're adults.

The growing-up years are volatile for the children. Nelda continually threatens suicide and often seems threatened by her own children. "She wanted to keep us at her emotional level," Vivian says.

In one of her darker periods, Nelda resorts to placing the children in an orphanage. She takes them out, puts them in again. "We were institutionalized at her hands," Vivian explains. "All of these things we excused and forgave and excused and forgave."

Nelda is an intelligent woman, but she does not follow through on treatment or therapy for her mental health problems. As a defense mechanism, she sabotages relationships. If she does not let people close to her, the logic goes, she won't be hurt. "She just didn't have any confidence in herself at all," Paula says.

Georgia Tann's evil legacy passes down through generations, as these five children of an angry adoptee stolen from her yard, know all too well.

Occasionally she would hit her children in anger, with a belt or a hairbrush, or smack them on the fanny. Meanwhile, the siblings take on parenting roles, sometimes parenting their mother, sometimes one another. Vivian says, "I felt very maternal with my sisters."

Tragically, their brother dies by suicide at age thirty-four, unable to surmount issues that ranged from drug and alcohol abuse to business problems. "My mother modeled that that was the way out of pain," Vivian says. "My first feeling was 'At least now he's at peace.'"

As the youngest, Kate was the closest to their mother and speaks more gently about her. "My mother had a lot of issues," she says. "She was ill for a very long time . . . She had to bring five children up on her own, so she was a hard worker. She was very smart."

If there is one thing these sisters learned from Nelda, it is that they did not want to pass this trauma on to the next generation. They yearned to do better with their own children. "I saw my mother early on as a model to be opposite to," Vivian says.

"I learned to take care of my children and grandchildren and hold them close," Paula adds. Her daughter loved her grandmother Nelda. "If anyone loved my mother, it was her grandchildren," she says. "They didn't have the history with her. She didn't hurt them the way she hurt us."

Kate agrees: "She spent a lot of time being a grandmother, which she loved."

For Elinor, the second to youngest, the journey was harder. "I did what my mother did. I got pregnant at sixteen, but I made a different choice than my mother." Knowing that she was not capable of raising a child at that young age, Elinor planned to give her baby up for adoption. Her mother, though, wanted to raise the baby, and she took Elinor to a rare counseling session in an attempt to convince her to keep the child.

"I made that choice," Elinor says; she wanted to spare her child an upbringing similar to her own. "I put her up for adoption, which was very painful." Thirty years later she was reunited with that daughter, who was herself a new mother by then. "We have a really beautiful relationship," Elinor tells me.

She and her daughter have come full circle: beauty from ashes, joy from pain, healing from heartbreak, strength from suffering. In so many ways, that is the story of these four strong women, left to deal with the aftermath of that long-ago ride in Tann's black limousine.

A small packet of tissues makes its way around the table. We make ample use of them as the sisters recount this story of three generations having been handed an heirloom no one wants. "It's part of the healing process," says Vivian, sixty-five when we meet. "Our mother talked about this all the time . . . Till the day she died, she was miserable and angry about this."

"She always felt lost without her family," Kate says. "She remembered them."

Since reading the novel, they have researched their mother's family history more and begun to talk about it publicly. Although they're now spread apart, in Florida, Arkansas, New Jersey, and Pennsylvania, their individual stories are similar.

They open themselves in vulnerable ways as they talk, often seeming to fit a missing piece into their puzzle as we visit. "We still are clearly working through the trauma," Elinor, sixty, says.

"This has been an opportunity for all of us to be together," Paula, sixty-two, points out. "We don't often do that." She looks around the table: four sisters together, just like the four sisters in Lisa's novel. Paula remembers her mother once more: "I think she would have gotten great joy out of us coming to Memphis."

The sisters are alike in many ways—earnest, smart, introspective, respectful of one another, clearly affected by their upbringing. And surprisingly, there's something else they share: yoga. Each of them came to her own version of yoga as a girl, using it to escape a chaotic home life. "As individuals, I think we each found yoga to be extremely therapeutic," Vivian says. "I remember doing stretches that I had no idea were yoga." Three of the sisters teach yoga, and two travel to teach it around the world.

They have been close throughout the years, though with the tense periods that often accompany relationships between sisters. They've always looked for ways to heal. From the time they learned to talk, they rehashed Nelda's stories, trying to make sense of her. "We commiserated forever," Vivian says. "My mother was a real challenge. She was a difficult person to get along with."

And much of that difficulty must be laid at Georgia Tann's doorstep. The trauma she set in motion affected multiple generations. Now it is a still-open wound slowly being stitched together by an understanding and acceptance of what happened, and by knowing this has happened to other families, too. Theirs is not the only family. Not by a long shot.

"Reading the book touched me so much," Paula says. "I had so much more compassion for my mother . . . I wanted to find out more."

She is the first one to have come across *Before We Were Yours*. She describes how it happened.

PAULA AND A GROUP of friends get together monthly at one another's houses to discuss a book. They are looking for a new read and notice *Before We Were Yours* on the *New York Times* bestseller list. As someone reads the description, Paula gasps, "Oh my gosh! This is the story of my mother."

Her friends are shocked.

When Paula gets home, she calls Vivian. "My book club is reading this book," she says. "It's all about what happened to Mom."

Reading the novel is an emotional experience for Paula. "When I finished it, I felt drained," she says. "It was like a revelation coming over me. This is what really happened." Her book club is stunned. "They just cannot believe it happened and that they know someone who's been through this."

Vivian, busy with her work as a yoga teacher and other activities in Florida, more or less forgets the book after Paula tells her about it . . . until former first lady Laura Bush, one of her yoga students who has become a close friend, mentions *Before We Were Yours* to her. Years earlier, the first lady heard bits and pieces of Vivian's story and was fascinated by it. She even insisted that Vivian share the story with the former president. "Tell George your story," she said.

Vivian hesitated. "It was so rare that I told the story. Thinking about it so much is really recent." She remembers that former president George W. Bush listened politely. "Laura was pivotal over the next few years in encouraging me to voice it more and more," she says. Vivian's story becomes an intimate bit of knowledge the two share, a building block of their friendship. In early 2018, Laura is leaving Florida for Texas and says, almost offhandedly, "You know, that book is on the *New York Times* bestseller list. I'm going to get it."

"Then I will, too," Vivian agrees.

She contacts Lisa before she reads the novel. In the email, she explains the basics of her mother's story and a hint of the generational suffering that is the unwanted legacy shared by so many of the families affected by Tann's adoption business. She thanks Lisa for bringing the TCHS history into the open. "I am the daughter of one of the stolen children, and my life and the lives of my siblings were very much impacted by my mother's experience in Tennessee," she writes in the email.

Then she reads the novel. "It was my mother's story," she recounts with no small degree of amazement. "I mean, *my* mother's story."

She repeats those words to her own book club after they

read the novel. She has read articles and seen the TV movie *Stolen Babies*. But after reading the novel, she can only wonder, *How* could this possibly happen?

Others echo her sentiments. They are equally appalled that such a thing could be allowed to go on . . . and for decades.

In May—with the reunion planned for early June—Vivian receives the email about the gathering. She is in the middle of plans surrounding her son's college graduation and is not sure she can make it happen. Still, she sends emails to her sisters and an uncle and tells them she is going.

Her first call is from Paula. Then Kate. Elinor texts, not planning to attend. But then she decides she wants to visit with her sisters. She is the one most conflicted about coming to Memphis. "I had mixed feelings," she says. "Out of my three sisters, I've been the least interested in the actual history. I had to go through a process to decide. I felt very grateful that I had made the decision."

Despite work, expenses, and logistical challenges, the sisters make it happen. Paula, who doesn't trust easily, and Kate fly out of Philadelphia together—the same city that Nelda arrived in by train all those years ago. "I was excited." Paula pauses. "I was a little apprehensive." When they land, she thinks, *We're here. This is going to help me.*

And here in the midst of our weekend, they're finding out that it has.

"I felt guilt and responsibility and shame, as if my family were so much worse than anyone else's," Vivian admits. As she tells her story—more often and in more depth than she ever has before—she begins to feel the effect. "It's interesting that I'm sharing that without tears," she says. "How healing it is to tell that story without guilt and shame."

Kate started reading *Before We Were Yours* the day Vivian told her about it. "It is a part of our history," she points out.

For Elinor, the novel initiated a deeper understanding of what their mother suffered. "I think that all of us had a tremendous amount of shame because of how unstable our mother was," she says, growing somber at the thought.

Paula sums up what each of her sisters has said in her own words, at one point or another during our conversation: "I didn't understand what she went through. She wasn't easy to live with, so I didn't want to *know* what she went through." She considers her words, and then, decisively, she adds, "I wish Mother were here—to know that people are trying to know more about it."

THE WEEKEND CONTAINS ONE more emotional tribute to Nelda; it takes place prior to our visit at the hotel. On their first evening in Tennessee, the sisters head to the Mississippi River. Down on the riverbank, so similar to the place where their mother was stolen all those years ago, they say a prayer together.

At first, Paula is not interested in being part of the river ceremony. But then her feelings change. "It wasn't really until I was there, and we did it," she reflects, "that I felt it was the best place for her. Her roots were there. She was back home."

"This was really what she wanted," Kate says. "I feel like I brought her home, and that made me happy."

Elinor climbs down to the water's edge, carrying the small urn containing their mother's ashes. This detail does not pass unnoticed by her siblings, since she was, perhaps, the sister most often in conflict with Nelda. As she opens the container and lets her mother's ashes float into the air and the water, she forgives her, and asks for her forgiveness. "I really felt at peace that I was able to do that," she says when we talk back at the hotel. "I feel like I understood before she died that the hatred and conflict weren't personal. She was just afraid of life and everyone."

"You're back home," Elinor murmurs. They have brought their mother full circle.

THE LESSON OF
FORGIVENESS

————

Despite the heaviness of the sisters' story, I don't leave the conference room emotionally spent. I come away from my conversation with these four women feeling hopeful.

The reunion is doing unexpectedly good things—not just for the attendees but for everyone it touches. Connections are formed. Friendships made. I hear details being shared with the hotel staff at the desk, with other guests, with people at book talks and gatherings.

We are moving toward the final events of our time together, which include a Sunday morning trip to the historic cemetery to pay tribute to those who died at the hands of people entrusted to care for them, babies whose lives were lost at the Tennessee Children's Home Society in Memphis.

Forgiveness has been much mentioned during the last few days, yet I find it hard to forgive Tann and equally hard to forgive those who helped her in courtrooms, on country roads, and in boardinghouses where desperate young women needed help.

I hope that had I been there, I would have had the courage to use my journalism skills to shine the light of truth on the situation. But that lets me off the hook too easily. In my life today, I have the same responsibility: to speak out when wrong is done. We all do.

We have to pay attention, raise our voices, have compassion, do good.

Because I'm about to visit a place that shows what happens when no one insists loudly enough that something is very wrong.

PART FOUR

The Reckoning

Their final peace a blessing.

—FROM THE MONUMENT TO CHILDREN
WHO DIED AT THE HANDS OF THE
TENNESSEE CHILDREN'S HOME SOCIETY

CHAPTER 19

A HISTORIC CEMETERY
AND FINAL PEACE

———

"I could be right there under that tree."

A DRAMATIC SPAN BRIDGE LEADS INTO HISTORIC ELMWOOD Cemetery in Memphis.

One moment you are on an industrial city street; the next you're looking out at the final resting places of some of the most famous and infamous citizens of Tennessee. The scene is a mixture of park and graveyard, framed by fifteen hundred majestic oaks, magnolias, and other ancient trees.

On this summer Sunday, everything feels symbolic. Sacred, even.

A bridge. The perfect metaphor for what has happened this weekend in our lives. The past and the present have become, in some way, connected. This final day is intended for those two afternoon book talks that set this entire plan into motion less than three months ago, but today is also for reflection, for wrapping up . . . and for saying goodbye in more ways than one. Only a train in the distance interrupts the quiet as we arrive at the cemetery early in the morning to pay a visit before the schedule becomes too chaotic. Even the birds sound politely subdued as we enter. The sky is Tennessee summer blue with the occasional cotton-white cloud. Sun-dappled leaves shadow the path we seek.

The historical Elmwood Cemetery is a reminder that while many TCHS adoptees have died, their lives have mattered. "Our stories live on," says Lisa Wingate, speaking at the cemetery during the reunion ceremony.

The past greets us here, prepared to stir up memories, questions, emotions. All the players in the strange saga of the Tennessee Children's Home Society are represented in some way.

Among those buried beneath these stones are crooked politicians and wealthy patrons who allowed Georgia Tann and the Tennessee Children's Home Society to prosper from the lives of innocent children. Tann herself is not here; she was buried in central Mississippi, her native state. I'm glad she is far from this day. She cannot lay her hands on it.

We are here to remember those better than she. The spirits we seek belong to angels.

An Elmwood Cemetery lane winds its way past both elaborate and simple headstones. The graveyard was founded in 1852 way out in the countryside, to give people a pastoral place where they could retreat from the hustle and bustle of city life. In more than a century, the city has crept near, but the original idea of a gardenlike setting remains. Approximately eighty thousand people are buried here in this historic nonprofit cemetery, safe under the watchful eyes of executive director Kim Bearden, who has run it for the past twenty years.

We are here to see only one grave. A resting place that cradles many lives and represents many more.

Nineteen babies registered by Tann as having died in the care of TCHS lie here, their deaths recorded between September 17, 1923, and December 10, 1949. Only nineteen of the five hundred estimated to have died in the care of her system of unregulated boardinghouses and the notorious Receiving Home on Poplar Avenue are remembered here. The monument on the TCHS lot was erected just three years ago, after a historian discovered the communal plot in the cemetery's record books. He pointed out the shame of the graves having gone unmarked for decades, the children, once more, forgotten. The cemetery raised donations to pay for a proper marker.

Under the spreading arms of a nearby magnolia tree, this piece of earth feels hallowed.

Lisa, three of our adoptees, and I emerge from our cars. The almost-citrus scent of large white magnolia blossoms hangs in the air as we pause, our eyes on the piece of stone that says so much. A carved marble angel watches over this piece of land.

The words chiseled into the stone bring a chill on a hot day:

THE TENNESSEE CHILDREN'S
HOME SOCIETY

AN INFAMOUS HISTORY. A TRAGIC LEGACY.
SEPTEMBER 17, 1923–DECEMBER 10, 1949
IN MEMORY OF THE 19 CHILDREN WHO FINALLY
REST HERE. UNMARKED IF NOT UNKNOWN.
AND OF ALL THE HUNDREDS WHO DIED UNDER
THE COLD, HARD HAND OF THE TENNESSEE
CHILDREN'S HOME SOCIETY. THEIR FINAL RESTING
PLACE UNKNOWN. THEIR FINAL PEACE A BLESSING.

THE HARD LESSON OF
THEIR FATE CHANGED
ADOPTION PROCEDURE AND LAW NATIONWIDE.

Tears pool in the eyes of the adoptees. Lisa and I are shaken, and I hang back. Photographer Cindy, her husband, and a two-person video crew here to capture this moment have turned solemn. The three adoptees and Lisa clasp hands and approach the marker, which sits among other graves on a small rise, not all that noticeable unless you are looking for it.

They read the words softly. Touch the stone. Exhale. They quietly ask the familiar question, the same one I'm thinking: *How could this have happened?*

The why and the how of it, as always.

After a few moments, they speak, haltingly, fervently.

"There but for the grace of God go I," Janie says softly, perhaps remembering lying in Tann's main Receiving Home at three and a half years old, a malnourished little blond girl given juice and a vitamin and left to survive a bout with tonsillitis . . . or not.

Patricia, whom I interviewed in Georgia, joins us on Face-Time. Even four hundred miles away, she is moved, and she speaks of the ancient magnolia tree over the monument. "It's so sheltering and protecting," she says. Perhaps she, too, is considering the deplorable condition she was in when she was delivered to that kitchen in New York City and she pulled herself onto the pant leg of her new father . . . and into his heart. Things could have gone much differently. "All they didn't get when they were alive," she continues. Even from such a distance, she shares the intensity of our feelings in this sacred place.

Connie, who set this gathering in motion, is tearful. "It has been my dream to get together," she says. When she sent that first email ten months ago, asking about a reunion, how could she have known we would wind up in this spot on this day? How could anyone have known?

"Thank God you're all here," Lisa says. She doesn't mean *here*, now, in this place. She means here, at all. In this *world*. Any one of these incredible, vibrant women could be among those tiny victims. Another life unrealized.

All those children. Hundreds of tragically short lives. All that potential. Just . . . *gone*.

The realities of what happened at TCHS are hard to contemplate, but they are necessary to revisit. The history we deny is the history we are most likely to repeat.

Each of the women places a white rose on the marker.

Although the clock has not yet reached ten, the air hangs heavy. The emotions and the steamy humidity sap our energy. The core group shares some final thoughts, a few people touch the stone again, and then we depart, leaving behind a wish that echoes the last words on the reverse side of the stone.

That all children will be loved.

Lillian, who lives across town, prepares to make her own pilgrimage to the memorial in a few hours. Even though she has lived not far from here her entire life, she has never visited it before, never seen this monument to babies who, like herself, lay sick and untended in TCHS cribs but found no champion to rescue them.

When she arrived in the early afternoon, with a friend and a cemetery docent, the sight hit her hard, she tells me a little while later in the cemetery chapel. Were it not for Viola and Harold, who rescued a seriously ill infant girl, she quite likely could have been buried here. Or somewhere else, anonymously. Her emotions pour forth as she, a survivor, describes paying her respects to those who did not survive. She reflects on her life and Tann and the scandal. As she stood at the graveside, the reality was painful.

But there is grace. Hers was a life that was spared. A good life, and she has passed along that good to others.

When Lillian left the plot, she proceeded uphill to the beautiful Lord's Chapel, with its soaring, arched glass windows. The sun had shifted in the sky, and massive trees shaded the graves beyond.

Now the mood inside the small space vibrates with the anticipation of the shoulder-to-shoulder crowd, the enthusiasm of executive director Kim, and the newfound camaraderie of a group of adoptees who didn't know one another forty-eight hours ago. Now they sit in the front row together, chatting, linked by memories of days long past and their fresh friendships, while I stand in the back and watch in awe.

Kim introduces Lisa to the volunteer who first discovered the unmarked TCHS graves and campaigned for a monument. While I wait for the program to start, a member of the cemetery staff takes me over to look at plot maps that show who is buried in the grave, children known only by their first names. Kim also connects me with Shirley Farnsworth of Memphis, who donated most of the money for the marker. She did it in memory of her daughter, Cynthia, who died at birth in 1963. "It took me a long time to be able to do something to honor my child," she says. "After all those years, it was something to do for my baby and those babies."

An angel sits atop the monument dedicated to children who died while in the care of Georgia Tann.

A journalist from the Memphis *Commercial Appeal*, the local daily newspaper, shows up and stakes out a spot near me in the back of the crowded room. "We didn't even advertise this event," Kim says. "So many of you were so interested in the book . . . That's the power of this story."

Lisa stands to start things off. "This whole front row is filled with adoptees from the Tennessee Children's Home Society," she says. "This is the crazy reality of what happened here in Memphis. Money and power made things happen. Why didn't people say something? We all have to be that person who is *there*, who speaks up. Be that one person for one person."

She talks about her novel, reads a selection from Rill's story, but then she cuts her planned remarks short and looks at the group of adoptees in front of her. This day in this place is about them. She invites them to turn their chairs around and speak if they would like to.

The crowd's energy sizzles as it leans in to hear comments from Connie, James, Lillian, and Janie. The stories told haltingly on Friday at Kirby Pines now come more easily, with a smattering of jokes and an oddly lighthearted moment when they compare their adoption prices. The conversation, though sad, shows the power of claiming their truth and of finding a tribe of people who know what it means to have come through TCHS. This is, in many ways, a moment of triumph.

When James mentions that he will meet blood relatives in an hour, he falters. The weekend has been so full and so meaningful for him. His daughter, Brigette, stands and tearfully looks toward Lisa, then moves nearer to her father.

"Seeing the plot here really hit me hard," she says. "He was in the care of the Georgia Tann home as a preemie." She has steered this journey through many hard moments. "I'm not sure why it's taken us so long," she says, "but I believe things have come together for a reason."

Brigette recalls her dad, who started looking for his family when she was one year old, telling her when she was a girl about Tann and the sale of babies. Now the story has come to life. "I think there's a feeling in all of us to want to know our roots," she says. "We want to know our history and what led up to us."

Questions pour forth. The members of the audience shift even closer to the edges of their seats.

Lillian, a Memphian like most in the crowd, grabs their attention when she quietly sums up the horrors of TCHS. "I could be right there under that tree," she says as she looks out the window toward the grave, which lies just down the hill.

A hush falls over the room, a stark realization. The truth can, at times, be both sharp-edged and beautiful. As the program ends, the crowd stays. A book club lines up to take a photograph with Lisa. The reporter interviews Lillian. Two women, seated near the front, catch my eye, and I speak to them. The daughters of an adoptee, a man now eighty-one and in poor health, they learned much about their father's history after reading *Before We Were Yours*. They knew he was adopted in Memphis but did not know the details. "We need to find out where you came from," they told him.

Their adoptive grandmother had informed them that their father came from a wealthy family. "Granddaddy didn't like to talk about it," one sister says. "If you mentioned the word *orphanage*, Granddaddy would get mad."

After reading the novel, they wrote for their father's adoption paperwork, which arrived at Thanksgiving time, five months after *Before We Were Yours* came out. The sisters did not open the packet of papers; instead, they gave it to their ailing father. "These are your adoption papers," they said to him. Their father tore into the envelope, and together they read his birth name. "Daddy," one daughter said, "that was your name."

He was born in May 1936 and adopted two days later, given one name at birth and another by his new parents. His birth mother was sixteen, and his biological grandmother wanted to keep him. His father was twenty-one or twenty-two and did not want anything more to do with the girl or the baby.

I introduce the sisters to Lisa, and they visit, and then they and I step outside the chapel, where they spread photographs on a stone bench. The crowd swirls around us, but we are in a bubble underneath a tree, lost in the past.

The details are familiar and yet different, achingly sad. After the teen mother gave up her son, she wrote Tann and asked how her "friend" was and if Tann thought he might be returned. In a surprisingly reassuring typewritten letter, Tann replied, "Our little friend is doing beautifully. He has a lovely home and the people are devoted to him." This exchange, a teenager wondering about her baby, using the code "little friend," hoping he is well and loved, is hard for me to process.

The sisters are not inclined to attempt to connect with other relatives. "They probably don't know anything about Daddy," one says. "We don't want to disrupt their families." Then she continues: "I do want to find out about his mother. I want to know if she had more children."

Her sister jumps in: "I'd like to know if she had a good life."

Their father's memory is failing, they tell me, and this new information flits in and out of his mind. He asks them, "What was my real name again?"

The women believe adoption was right for their father and gave him loving parents. "Daddy was so fortunate. They worshipped the ground he walked on," one of his daughters says. Then she pauses, her next words forced out: "I don't want Daddy to be forgotten."

This is the message Lisa has emphasized throughout the weekend. "The saddest thing is when our stories die with us," she says. "People so often say to me, 'I wish we'd written the family stories down.'"

Afternoon light shines through the floor-to-roof clear glass windows of the chapel, illuminating them. A hawk circles, gliding above the ghosts of the cemetery.

The sight feels like a benediction to the weekend.

Our emotions rise like the Mississippi River after a torrential rain as we prepare to part. Hugs and phone numbers and promises to visit are exchanged.

Despite two dozen reasons why the reunion should not have worked, we have come together, and we have been changed. The adoptees have embraced a shared past. They've talked with others like them, some for the first time. They've vented their anger at what the Tennessee Children's Home Society, under Tann's dictatorship, did to their lives, the families of their generation, and those yet to come.

Their stories, remarkable and chilling, have spread out like the limbs of the most expansive oak in this graceful cemetery. They've been told to residents of a retirement home and exchanged in the hospitality suite and over wine in individual rooms, at the library, in a bookstore, at the cemetery, and in the chapel.

These people are so much more than survivors, as we described them in the weeks before we met them, when our unlikely plans wavered into existence. These people are heroes. They own a piece of history. They have children and grandchildren and enough happy memories to shove Tann and TCHS to the side. This weekend, they triumphed and told their stories, in their own voices. Those stories have power. They connect people. They heal. They teach in the telling. In the listening, in the writing, and in the reading.

Lillian's revelation hangs in the air around us: "Georgia Tann had left me to die, but I'm seventy-one years old, and I'm still here." Still here. This small group of an unlikely club is still here.

"I never expected to bring together people who lived this story," Lisa says. "This weekend has been a completely unexpected thing. These stories matter."

CHAPTER 20

AFTERWARD

---

*We need to be given peace and freed of the misery
that comes from not knowing, and allowed to live with the
truth before we pass from this world.*

—LETTER FROM A TENNESSEE CHILDREN'S
HOME SOCIETY ADOPTEE TO HER UNKNOWN
BIRTH FAMILY

ON THE WEEKEND WHEN WE GATHER, THE MEMPHIS STREETS symbolize the New South. The boll weevil has been largely eradicated. The shantyboats that peopled the riverbanks in the time of *Before We Were Yours* have long since faded from existence, victims of waterway legislation, multimillion-dollar lock-and-dam systems, and modern economics. Jim Crow laws that legalized segregation were overturned in the 1960s, and the city's population is nearly two-thirds African American. Landmarks such as Graceland, Elvis Presley's former home; the National Civil Rights Museum; historic Beale Street, with its blues music; and the Memphis Pyramid draw tourists by the tens of thousands. Beyond that, Tennessee has some of the most stringent adoption laws in the country, and throughout the country, adoption has lost the stigma it held for past generations. Georgia Tann has been dead for nearly seventy years.

Connie

CONNIE TRAVELS TO THE AIRPORT LATE ON SUNDAY AFTERNOON after the TCHS reunion she'd imagined for so long has ended. She's headed back to the West Coast. Triumphant.

She did it.

"Have you ever considered doing a reunion?" that one reader asked her at a book club.

Connie responded, reached out to Lisa, and did a hundred things, from inviting attendees to negotiating room rates, to make it happen. She flew in late at night and got up early. She visited in person with others like her and helped make guests feel welcome.

Her idea gave something important to those from whom Tann took so much: not just the chance to speak their stories out loud but proof that people are interested in hearing what they have to say, that strangers care about this long-ago miscarriage of justice.

Connie has smiled much during the gathering, and she has shed tears. "This was so important to me personally," she affirms as we say goodbye.

Two other adoptees, friends now, take her to catch her flight. All three of them cry as they hug farewell. "We spent this wonderful weekend together," Connie says. "I was very sad to be leaving that group."

She chooses her words carefully, remembering the sweet moments as she tells me about all this when we talk later on the phone. "Getting everyone together and watching them deal with it, living it . . . comparing their prices . . ." We laugh together. We recall the teasing about how much each adoptee cost—dark humor, but humor nonetheless. The jokes cover deep emotions. "It's been healing, but it was also like having a jack-in-the-box jump out," she says. Now it will probably not go back in. Light shines on their stories, chases the shadows from dark places.

Connie tells me about sitting down at the airport bar and ordering a glass of wine, waiting for her flight out of Memphis. She is torn between the need to connect and a raw urge to be alone when two women sit beside her. They strike up a conversation, and Connie shares a few details about the weekend. It turns out that one of the women's aunts was adopted through TCHS.

Of course.

Countless families have a connection to the horror of Tann and those who let her operate until 1950, the year Connie was born. This is a story that doesn't have an ending. It never will. For thousands of families, tens of thousands of lives, it will always be part of their history.

When Connie settles into her airplane seat, she is exhausted. Departing Memphis is almost as hard as coming there was. "My biggest regret leaving was that I wanted to have more time with these people . . . I still think of those four girls," she says of the sisters who brought their mother's ashes to the river. "Those four girls are so lucky to have each other."

Back at home, Connie talks to her therapist about the reunion. The counselor exclaims, "This is the best thing that's ever happened to you!"

CONNIE IS NOT ALONE in her tangled mix of post-reunion elation and fatigue.

Janie

BACK IN ALABAMA, JANIE UNPACKS HER CAR, THEN LIES DOWN.
The gathering was fulfilling and exhausting. "It closed up sections in me where there had been holes," she confides. "It was very cleansing . . . A lot of things that other adoptees said touched me. I think we all made a bond . . . we all reached out."

She felt close to the others. "It was interesting to me and meaningful to share similar stories," she says. In small groups, they spent time considering where they would be if they hadn't been adopted. "It's interesting looking at the way our lives turned out."

She also uncovered an unexpected theme: "Something I learned this weekend that I don't think I would have ever learned was how many adoptees went into rough homes. So many homes had alcoholism or not a happy marriage or couldn't legally adopt . . . When we were sitting around talking, I kept hearing this same dysfunction. The more I hear, the more I realize that I'm not the only one . . . If I hadn't gone to Memphis for the reunion, I wouldn't have put this together."

She has overcome much to get to this place, and her response is simple: "Life takes care of us."

Lillian

THE ENTIRE WEEKEND TOUCHED LILLIAN. "I FELT AN INSTANT bond with these strangers," she says. Her story appears on the front page of the Memphis newspaper on the Monday after the cemetery event. "I've had a lot of reactions from friends and neighbors and more requests from book clubs," she says. She even heard from the half sister she found when she was fifty.

Stanley

A CONFUSING AND UPSETTING DEVELOPMENT SLAMS STANLEY after the reunion. A cousin finally locates a death certificate for Stanley's newborn brother, and he does not know what to make of it. "I wanted to let you know sooner," he says when I reach out to him, "but I just didn't know how to find the words . . . This whole thing still raises more questions for me. The date on the certificate was about six days later than my mother was told that the baby died."

His parents were not given the baby's body, and there is no record of a burial. *Others in the OB ward were told their babies had died, too, so were death certificates falsified and meted out over a period of days?*

Perhaps in the future, Stanley will find more answers, more peace. Maybe his brother, David, if he is alive, will submit his DNA for testing, and the family will be reunited.

Perhaps. Perhaps. Perhaps. The refrain is haunting.

Robert and Heather

FOR HEATHER AND HER FATHER, ROBERT, THAT SEVEN-DOLLAR baby delivered by limousine to rural Arkansas, the reunion is followed by a different kind of surprise.

"Just this week," Heather says when we chat a couple of months after meeting in Memphis, "Arkansas has opened its adoption records." So Heather's twenty-plus-year search for her family history will continue. She will do more research and see who they might discover out there. "It's a very strange feeling. We could find out they were very good people. There's a fear of the unknown."

That fear of the unknown likely drove Arkansas's reluctance to make certain records available to adult adoptees, and that fear is in part why many other states restrict access to records, allowing only nonidentifying information, if any. Even obtaining something as basic as an adoptee's original birth certificate requires a court order in some states. But my TCHS interviews have shown me that a large number of adoptees hunger for their personal information, and their medical history in particular. Birth parents may feel differently, however, and laws generally allow birth parents to decide whether they want to connect with their biological children and whether that contact must be made through an intermediary.

I was not surprised to learn that since Missouri, another of Tennessee's neighbors, opened its records in 2016, the state's residents have battled a long waiting list to access their original birth certificates.

How things have changed since Denny Glad and her volunteers tirelessly traveled to small-town courthouses to write information on index cards. Nowadays, tenacious TCHS adoptees are finding birth-family connections with the help of popular and easy DNA tests, the Internet, and the reach of social media sites such as Facebook.

Whatever Heather and Robert find in the records, the reunion moved them ahead on their journey. "It was kind of like being a member of a strange club. It was genuine, and it was safe," Heather says. "I just appreciate it and enjoyed meeting the people and hearing their stories . . . I'd love to hear more stories."

James and Brigette

THROUGHOUT THE REUNION, JAMES, HIS WIFE, MILLIE, AND their daughter, Brigette, are excited and a little tense about their first meeting with members of James's birth family. The rest of us share their emotions and wonder what will happen after they leave us at the cemetery on that Sunday afternoon. James is such a sweet soul, and none of us can bear to think that he might be hurt by relatives who do not know him. Still, given the way the TCHS reunion has gone, we feel hopeful as they leave us to travel to the restaurant chosen as the site for their family meeting.

Such an event was unthinkable about a year and a half before the reunion, until James decided to have his DNA analyzed. From that, Brigette found cousins who live way down South, a world away from their own home in Utah. Then the TCHS reunion cropped up. "The timing was really good," James says. "So many things came together to make it work."

The nerves, as it turns out, aren't necessary. He and his cousins connect in a way that kinfolks do, talking about their lives, their interests, their similar experiences jumping out of airplanes in Vietnam, and even the birth names they share. "We hit it off like you wouldn't believe," James tells me afterward, with a kind of mystified glee. "We kind of look alike. It's amazing. We had an absolutely wonderful, wonderful experience with them."

Brigette exudes happiness—and maybe a dash of relief— when she calls me after I speak with her father. "It was really easy. My dad shook everyone's hand. He sat between cousins, and they just talked and talked and talked." After dinner, with the restaurant too loud for the conversations they wanted to have, they were invited to a cousin's home. "I wish I had cooked for y'all," one cousin's wife, all Southern hospitality, said.

"They weren't standoffish," Brigette says. "They were totally down to earth and wanting to talk." Brigette can scarcely believe what has improbably come together. There she is, late on a summer Sunday evening, visiting her father's birth family. "I'm in a living room in Mississippi, of all places."

The week after James gets back from his odyssey, he speaks to a genealogy class at his church. "I think it's important families find out about their families," he says. "You want to know who you belong to."

Brigette addresses the entire congregation for Father's Day. "We believe that we were put on this earth to make choices," she says. "My dad had to make a lot of choices." James expresses joy that he made the hard choice to take the trip. "It was one of the highlights of my life to meet those wonderful people and know I'm related to them." Leaving Tennessee was a little sad, though. "I've been there now," he says. "It was a magnificent experience that I'll cherish the rest of my life."

Brigette hopes there may be more family reunions ahead and answers to other questions. "My dad's story is not yet finished," she says.

Vivian, Paula, Elinor, and Kate

THE FOUR SISTERS RETURN TO THEIR SEPARATE PARTS OF THE country, each of them wrapped up in thoughts about the weekend.

As Kate's plane lifts off, she is joyful. The reunion connections run deep, and she feels a sense of kinship with those she met. "It's been a very good learning experience for me to listen to the other stories," she observes, "and it brought us together as a family . . . and we brought our mother home."

Vivian emphasizes the value of remembering: "It's important that this story not be forgotten for its reverberations and trickle-down effects."

Paula agrees as we discuss writing these stories down. "Do something so this doesn't happen again," she urges.

Nelda's daughters are determined to discover as many relatives as they can.

"Now I'm in touch with a brand-new first cousin," Vivian says. "Guess what? She lives in Memphis. I wish we had known that, and I'm going to follow up on it."

Paula tells her book-club friends all that she learned about Tann and TCHS. "They just can't believe it," she relates later, "how horrific it was. They can't believe it happened." She reflects on her time down South. "Coming back to my mother's roots was really coming back to *our* roots. Hearing the stories was heartwarming and emotional . . . The gathering really meant a lot to me . . . I've had to digest it all."

Elinor echoes the emotion: "I feel like I'm finally at a place where I can put the past to rest." Days after the weekend in Memphis, she takes a camping trip for her birthday, goes for long walks, and gradually processes the gathering. "I felt at peace. I also felt grateful."

The sisters plan to return to Memphis for their own summer reunion with birth-family members.

Perhaps other adoptees and their families will come back, too. "I would like to see it become an annual meeting," Kate says. "I just hope this continues and that it develops into something that brings closure to people before they pass away."

Lisa and Me

LISA AWAKENS EARLY ON MONDAY TO FLY TO CALIFORNIA TO give a book talk. She will scarcely mention the reunion; it is too fresh. But it will weigh on her mind as she settles into yet another airline seat. Her husband loads their car and heads toward Arkansas to pick up their dog and get a break from the delivery—and rapid-fire consumption—of endless takeout in our rooms.

My husband, super errand-runner and encourager, and I drive the twelve hundred miles to our new home in Colorado, happy to unwind together in the car. We discuss the wonderful people we met and the stories they so bravely shared. When I return to my office, I look through the notebooks filled with scrawled memories. I methodically label each interview, all of them carefully recorded in my notebooks, on my iPhone, or on my tiny digital recorder. Piles of paper begin stacking up, ranging from a copy of Georgia Tann's death certificate to my own copy of the Browning Report, which catalogs the results of attorney Taylor's investigation. Sticky notes dot every surface: Check on this. Look up that.

A flurry of emails, texts, and calls fly among all of us. The reunion continues. Our tie is strong.

The hope carried by these new friends wraps Lisa and me in its cloak as we gather at my house in July to consider what we have learned and to try to figure out how to encapsulate this odyssey we've been on. The kind souls we met remind me of the fictional adoptees in *Before We Were Yours* and the character

Avery's realization: "The five little river gypsies who suffered at the hands of the Tennessee Children's Home Society deserve to have their stories carried forward into the future."

It is not hard to see why these real-life people connected with the fictional Foss family. Fact has indeed met fiction. As I ponder this, I reflect on another quote from the novel that has especially resonated with me since our gathering, this one from the character May as she nears the end of her days: "People don't come into our lives by accident." Lisa and I agree that this seems especially true when we consider the group of people who traveled to the reunion, the messages they brought, and the stories we all took back home with us.

Perhaps somewhere, somehow, siblings will find one another through these and countless other stories. Or adoption laws will be changed in more states to allow families to reconnect. Maybe individual crusaders will step forth to make sure that nothing like this happens again. Perhaps yet another teenager somewhere will send in his DNA sample and find a long-lost relative for a grandparent.

Maybe after reading these stories, someone out there will choose to become that one person for one person. Change a life. Save a life.

Tell a story that would have otherwise been lost.

ACKNOWLEDGMENTS

THE GREATEST PLEASURE OF THIS BOOK HAS BEEN GETTING to know the wonderful people who shared their stories with us. We thank you for your generosity, the time you spent with us, and your friendship. We look forward to many visits ahead. Our gratitude also goes to all the people who hosted us in Memphis, including volunteer Janice and the entire welcoming group at Kirby Pines Retirement Community; the staff at Benjamin L. Hooks Central Library; our friends at Novel bookstore; Kim Bearden and her team at Elmwood Cemetery; and the staff of Staybridge Suites Memphis–Poplar Ave East, who went the extra mile to make our reunion group feel at home. And, of course, we thank photographer Cindy "Cuz" Self and her husband, Doug, and our intrepid husbands, Paul and Sam. Gratitude goes, too, to Lisa's mother, Sharon, and journalist friend Kathie Rowell for feedback and support of all kinds.

On the print and publishing side of things, thank you to our wonderful agent, Elisabeth Weed, who believed us when we said, "No, really, we're going to find a way to tell these stories." Our gratitude also goes to the publishing group at Penguin Random House and our dream team at Ballantine Books, including Kara Welsh, Kim Hovey, Jennifer Hershey, Matthew Martin, Susan Corcoran, Melanie DeNardo, Debbie Aroff, Toby Ernst, Jennifer Garza, Colleen Nuccio, Craig Adams, Bonnie Thompson, Barbara Bachman, and Emily Hartley— and especially to awesome editor Susanna Porter, who raced down the fast track with us to bring this book to print. Without the hard work and encouragement of all of you, these true stories might never have been told, and we hope that they do a good thing in the world and in the lives of vulnerable children today.

PHOTO CREDITS

ABOUT THE AUTHORS

JUDY CHRISTIE is an award-winning journalist and the author of eighteen books of both fiction and nonfiction. A former editor at daily newspapers in Tennessee, Louisiana, Florida, and Indiana, she holds a master's degree in literature from Louisiana State University in Shreveport. She and her husband live in rural Colorado.

judychristie.com

Facebook.com/JudyChristieAuthor

Twitter: @judypchristie

LISA WINGATE is a former journalist, an inspirational speaker, and the author of numerous novels, including the #1 *New York Times* bestseller *Before We Were Yours* and the national bestseller *Tending Roses*. She is a three-time ACFW Carol Award winner, a Christy Award nominee, an Oklahoma Book Award finalist, and a Southern Book Prize winner. She lives with her husband in Texas.

lisawingate.com

Facebook.com/LisaWingateAuthorPage

Twitter: @LisaWingate

Instagram: @author_lisa_wingate

This book was set in a Monotype face called Bell. The Englishman John Bell (1745–1831) was responsible for the original cutting of this design. The vocations of Bell were many—bookseller, printer, publisher, typefounder, and journalist, among others. His types were considerably influenced by the delicacy and beauty of the French copperplate engravers. Monotype Bell might also be classified as a delicate and refined rendering of Scotch Roman.